THE CRITICS DEBATE
General Editor Michael Scott

The Critics Debate

General Editor Michael Scott

PUBLISHED TITLES:
Sons and Lovers Geoffrey Harvey
Bleak House Jeremy Hawthorn
The Canterbury Tales Alcuin Blamires
Tess of the d'Urbervilles Terence Wright
Hamlet Michael Hattaway
The Waste Land/Ash Wednesday
    Arnold P. Hinchliffe
Othello Peter Davison
Paradise Lost Margarita Stocker
King Lear Ann Thompson
The Tempest David Daniell
Coriolanus Bruce King
Blake:Songs of Innocence and Experience
    David W. Lindsay
The Winter's Tale Bill Overton
Gulliver's Travels Brian Tippett
The Great Gatsby Stephen Matterson
To The Lighthouse Su Reid
Protrait of a Lady/Turn of the Screw
    David Kirby
Hard Times Allen Samuels
Philip Larkin Stephen Regan
Measure for Measure T.F. Wharton
Wuthering Heights Peter Miles
The Metaphysical Poets Donald Mackenzie
Heart of Darkness Robert Burden

FURTHER TITLES ARE IN PREPARATION

WUTHERING HEIGHTS

Peter Miles

For Win and Mike, with love and in memory

© Peter Miles 1990

All rights reserved. No reproduction, copy or transmission of this publication may be made without written permission.

No paragraph of this publication may be reproduced, copied or transmitted save with written permission or in accordance with the provisions of the Copyright, Designs and Patents Act 1988, or under the terms of any licence permitting limited copying issued by the Copyright Licensing Agency, 90 Tottenham Court Road, London W1P 9HE.

Any person who does any unauthorised act in relation to this publication may be liable to criminal prosecution and civil claims for damages.

First published 1990 by
THE MACMILLAN PRESS LTD
Houndmills, Basingstoke, Hampshire RG21 2XS
and London
Companies and representatives
throughout the world

ISBN 0–333–38516–0 hardcover
ISBN 0–333–38517–9 paperback

A catalogue record for this book is available from the British Library.

Printed in Hong Kong

Reprinted 1991, 1993

Contents

Acknowledgements   6
General Editor's Preface   7
A Note on Text and References   9
*Introduction: Wuthering Heights: Popular Memory/
             Critical Debate*   10

Part One: Survey

    Reading Biography: the Body in the Library   15
    Sources: Perforations in Other Tanks   22
    Narrative: the Villain in the Chinese Box   30
    Writing/Erasing/Reading Sexuality   35
    A Novel is a Novel/is an Author/is a Reader   44

Part Two: Appraisal: *Wuthering Heights*: Passion and
                              Property

    Houses and Titles   51
    The Nameless Man   53
    A Cuckoo's History: the Landlord as Hero   61
    Patriarchy and its Anxieties   70
    The Divided Woman   80
    Unquiet Slumbers: Ghosts and Literacy   87

References   94
Index   101

Acknowledgements

MY THANKS are due to Alcuin Blamires and Allen Samuels for exchanging ideas about this series; also to Belinda Humfrey and Malcolm Smith, as Chairs of Victorian Studies at SDUC, for opportunities to deliver early fragments of this text to tolerant audiences at Lampeter and Gregynog. In that context I am also grateful to Philip Collins for his comments. To Michael Scott and Macmillan's editors I owe thanks for their elastic professional patience. To Kathy, whose home has been haunted by the ghosts of Cathy and Catherine for quite long enough, I owe thanks for advice, encouragement, and a great deal more.

Peter Miles

General Editor's Preface

OVER THE last few years the practice of literary criticism has become hotly debated. Methods developed earlier in the century and before have been attacked and the word 'crisis' has been drawn upon to describe the present condition of English Studies. That such a debate is taking place is a sign of the subject discipline's health. Some would hold that the situation necessitates a radical alternative approach which naturally implies a 'crisis situation'. Others would respond that to employ such terms is to precipitate or construct a false position. The debate continues but it is not the first. 'New Criticism' acquired its title because it attempted something fresh calling into question certain practices of the past. Yet the practices it attacked were not entirely lost or negated by the new critics. One factor becomes clear: English Studies is a pluralistic discipline.

What are students coming to advanced work in English for the first time to make of all this debate and controversy? They are in danger of being overwhelmed by the cross-currents of critical approaches as they take up their study of literature. The purpose of this series is to help delineate various critical approaches to specific literary texts. Its authors are from a variety of critical schools and have approached their task in a flexible manner. Their aim is to help the reader come to terms with the variety of criticism and to introduce him or her to further reading on the subject and to a fuller evaluation of a particular text by illustrating the way it has been approached in a number of contexts. In the first part of the book a critical survey is given of some of the major ways the text has been appraised. This is done sometimes in a thematic manner, sometimes according to various 'schools' or 'approaches'. In the second part the authors provide their own appraisals of the text from their stated critical standpoint, allowing the reader the knowledge of their own particular approaches from which their views may in turn be evaluated. The series therein hopes to introduce and to elucidate criticism of authors and texts being studied and to encourage participation as the critics debate.

Michael Scott

# A Note on Text and References

PAGE NUMBERS in round brackets refer to the World's Classics edition of *Wuthering Heights*, edited by Ian Jack (Oxford and New York, 1981), which reprints the authoritative Clarendon text of the novel.

Bibliographical details of critical studies mentioned in the text are listed in the References section.

Where more than one study by a particular author has been cited, references in the text differentiate between them by date of publication (and by 'a' or 'b' to differentiate within particular years). Page numbers in square brackets refer to the study immediately under discussion.

Introduction
'Wuthering Heights':
Popular Memory/
Critical Debate

FREQUENTLY adapted for children's editions and for film and television, *Wuthering Heights* has left an indelible mark on British consciousness. Mention of the novel's name or of its principal characters almost guarantees the evocation in most minds of the idea of a love story, a sense of landscape, or an atmosphere of storm and conflict. One scene, where Cathy and Heathcliff call each other's names from distant hillsides, seems especially deeply engraved in popular memory – the more intriguingly so for the fact that no such scene is directly presented anywhere in Emily Brontë's text.

That visual myth of *Wuthering Heights*, embodied in those yearning figures on the moors, has entered twentieth-century popular memory not only as shorthand for Emily Brontë's novel, but as a sign for romantic love itself – for a love which survives all difficulties and which through its strength and vision, and through the overriding value accorded it by the protagonists, transcends time and space to testify to the spiritual potential of humanity. Denied each other in life, the lovers' creation of a unique union in death announces the scale of their experience and gives them entry to a standard iconography of love alongside such exponent figures as Romeo and Juliet, and Antony and Cleopatra.

British culture has frequently revisited that image of Cathy and Heathcliff on the moors in reviewing its own changing values. Reworkings of the received idea of the novel in popular memory can be ephemeral, superficial, or aim merely at immediate humour, yet they may still be enlightening, and not least for their implicit confidence in the large audiences they address sharing an understanding of what is meant within the culture by 'Wuthering Heights'.

For example, in the popular culture of the last twenty years one group of voices (Kate Bush, Genesis) continued to redeploy *Wuthering Heights* as a sign inherently affirming romantic passion and idealistic aspiration. Other voices reworked the mythical scene through travesty: Monty Python's 'semaphore version' of *Wuthering Heights* (where Cathy and Heathcliff stiffly communicate by flags from their respective hill-tops), and Dave Allen's sketch where the lovers rush down from the hills to collide at full speed, emerged from a sexually revolutionised culture and a new degree of social mobility in which the idea of lovers separated by constraint, or driven to communicate by indirection, could appear as simply absurd – at least from the viewpoint, in Kingsley Amis's phrase, of an 'I Want It Now' society.

Conversely, William Wyler's famous Hollywood version of 1939 asked its audience to see nothing absurd in the division of lovers by circumstance or by moral and social constraint, and cinema audiences watched Laurence Olivier and Merle Oberon in *Wuthering Heights* with the same kind of sympathetic attention as they would shortly watch the trials of Humphrey Bogart and Ingrid Bergman in *Casablanca*, of Trevor Howard and Celia Johnson in *Brief Encounter*.

Whether to endorse, to satirise, or to exploit (as in recent advertisements showing the Cathy and Heathcliff of the moors transferring their passion to a brand of video-recorder), these revisitings – while scribbling short-term modulations of value over its surfaces – recognise the resilience of *Wuthering Heights* in popular memory as an icon of romantic love. In that respect, Wyler's adaptation was typical in single-mindedly focusing on Heathcliff and Cathy; one critic was so pleased that he declared the film 'poetically written as the novel not always was, sinister and wild as it was meant to be, far more compact dramatically than Miss Brontë had made it'. This is revealing, both for the assumption that the wild and the sinister is what *Wuthering Heights* is essentially 'about', and for bizarrely implying that some perfectly wild *Wuthering Heights* preceded, and was imperfectly rendered in, Emily Brontë's version. Recently Tom Winnifrith [1983] has indeed suggested that a shorter *Wuthering Heights* may well have been first submitted for publication: many critics would have preferred that hypothetical draft; Moser has not been alone in maintaining that the second generation of characters contradict 'the novel's true subject' [p. 2]. Yet even were Winnifrith's speculation proved just, readers and critics have often collaborated too readily with popular memory to privilege their ideal *Wuthering Heights*, even at the expense of Emily Brontë's text. Besides, other significances have been discerned in the novel's conclusion, a constructive rejection of Heathcliff [Allott, 1958], or the gain of a feminisation of relationship [Senf, p. 212], rather than just the negative of Hareton's 'symbolic emasculation' [Thompson, p. 74].

There is no denying that *Wuthering Heights* is a love story – or rather, something like three love stories; or indeed that it utilises elements of the ghost tale; or that it presents powerful feelings and actions; or that it is a 'poetic' text both in offering a rich verbal field, and in utilising a rhetoric dealing in primary images of life and death, Heaven and Hell, calm and storm.

Wuthering Heights, however, also has aspects which may attract someone, such as myself, interested in the social and historical contextualisation of writing within a broad model of cultural activity. This means confronting deeply entrenched critical acceptance of Emily Brontë's 'isolation from significant social and economic forces' [Barclay, 1974, p. 8] and even hostility towards the very idea of social and historical approaches to her novel (as also to the relevance of any ethical or moral concerns in the writing or reading of the text).

In the 'Survey' section of the present book I review, on a sampling basis, issues in biography and the mythicisation of Emily, source-studies, narratological matters, psychoanalytical approaches, and formalist and post-structuralist dealings with the text. As in the 'Appraisal', a consciousness of feminist argument should be apparent through these sections.

To clarify the stance of my 'Appraisal', however, I need to indicate my own dissatisfaction with the idea of writers and texts being isolated from 'significant social and economic forces'. No human life – in Haworth any more than in London or New York – has been isolated from such forces, which are 'known' less in theory than through being engaged with in living, as also in and through writing. Indeed, the studies of *Wuthering Heights* which I have personally found most stimulating (and which have influenced my 'Appraisal' most) are those, often Marxist – and increasingly feminist – which argue the social, historical and ideological relationships of the text: notably Kettle, Eagleton [1975], Gilbert and Gubar, Kavanagh.

Novelists may well choose not to deal programmatically with political or social issues; in writing, they may not be fully conscious of the social, economic or political resonances of the words, ideas and images they organise (and disorganise) in their texts. Yet writers cannot prevent their language speaking of its production through specific circumstances of community, education and occasion, their sense of human interaction deriving from their own experience and such experience as their culture envisages, their sensibility and values revealing relationships of allegiance and disaffiliation in relation to their own historically specific society. This is not to understand writing as producing a specular reflection of society, or as being crudely determined by its context of production, but as a historically specific phenomenon most rich in its relations at the moment of its production.

If resonance lies inert or invisible within texts, then something may be revealed about the ideological stance of the writing – and the relative lack of disturbance such texts offered readers. Conversely, texts' capacities to make visible the invisible, to allow an exposure of the implications of the 'normal', the 'ordinary', the 'commonsense' in, say, class and gender relations, may testify to modulations of ideology finding construction in and through the act of writing, the laying down of a map of intellectual and emotional pressure-points, of desires and rejections, within a lived society. Language is a social medium, guilty of the meanings and values (and the tensions) of the culture in which it is used; it is not redeployed – anywhere – without some play occurring in those meanings and values, and it is within the world of those meanings and values that the text is eventually read. Writers are thus both instruments and agents of language and culture, building with pre-shaped materials – and yet able to display the composition, to redesign the shape of those materials, through the act of constructing something new.

Unlike many contemporary students of writing, I still cling to authors, and to their social formation and biography, as being relevant to the reading and debating of texts. I well see the point and fruits of methodologies abandoning such concerns to focus upon reading as an existential process rather than as the act of some normative, 'common' or 'ideal' reader. I have taken much on board from such approaches. Yet in the urge to rediscover the flux of reading experiences, there may be overcompensation for criticism's past tendencies to homogenise readers into one politico-cultural model, and to allow ideas about authorial competence to dictate the limits of possible and permitted readings. As I have suggested, texts do outlive their authors' control and take on a more dynamic condition, a 'mode of existence', which may change kaleidoscopically through time, as a living culture – inside and outside the institutions of criticism – alters the functions of those texts [Foucault]. Any moment in a culture's history is typified by its reworking and repositioning of existing texts as much as by its production of new ones. Allusion to *Wuthering Heights* in a Margaret Atwood story about a young girl growing up occurs within a contemporary repossessing of women's writing by women writers which is quite different in its implications for its own culture from William Wyler's, or Lord David Cecil's or Monty Python's revisitings. In other hands, critical, creative or institutional, *Wuthering Heights* does continue to suggest, and to participate in, new constellations of cultural pattern, new constructions of value and belief.

Yet texts are available to define and redefine readers and cultures because this woman or that man sat down at that place, at that period, and under those conditions, to face the task and delight, the conscious and unconscious play, of writing those words for such audiences as they envisaged. If that matrix is not the end of a text and its readers, it remains for me a primary focus of debate. On any journey, knowing where you've come from is a prerequisite of knowing where you are.

PART ONE
SURVEY

Reading Biography: the Body in the Library

Throughout its history of debate, *Wuthering Heights* has attracted such epithets as 'extraordinary' and 'astonishing'. Such words also figure in a frequently perceived paradox turning upon the assumed uneventfulness, isolation and cultural deprivation of Emily Brontë's life as contrasted with the dynamism of her writing. For 140 years, as her most recent (and most judicious) biographer phrases it, the persistent question has been: 'How could a young woman without much formal education and with little experience of life produce such an extraordinary work as *Wuthering Heights*?' [Chitham, 1987, p. 1]. Paradoxes, however, may be most compelling for their ideological assumptions, in this case concerning the relationships of gender, class and region to the production of valued writing ('young woman'/'formal education'/'little experience of life') [see Eagleton, 1983]. As phrased, the question can arise out of an appreciation of the historical factors inhibiting the formation of writers within specific social groups, but, presented as a paradox to be wondered at, it may also imply an outlook assuming that 'extraordinary work' is normally produced by, say, formally educated men of some years who have seen a lot of the world.

In practice, the 'paradox' of Emily and her writing has often tended to be as neatly resolved as it has been constructed, not so much through any re-evaluation of social factors or deconstruction of ideological assumptions, as by recourse to ideas of romantic genius and of inspiration blowing 'where it listeth', which have in turn risked limiting, even fossilising, assessments of both Emily and her writing. (Chesterton, in one of the least helpful remarks in the history of criticism, observed that *Wuthering Heights* might have been written by an eagle' [*cit.* Hafley, p. 202].) The 'paradox' is frequently validated by myths about consumption as an illness, inhuman celebrations of the ethereal tubercular artist floating ambiguously between body and spirit, between flush and pallor, living out an enhanced sexuality and an intensified imaginative life in the shadow of death [see Sontag]. However, to hold reservations about how the 'paradox' of Emily's life has tended to be posed and resolved is certainly not to undermine the value of the continuing biographical project: rather it is to underwrite those versions of the project which seek to evade distortion by myth.

If Emily Brontë's biography seems to resemble a mystery without a body, it is because so little is reliably known of her. She died young, quite shortly after the publication of *Wuthering Heights*. Apart from manuscripts of her poetry, few other documents she wrote survive. Her letters and so-called diary-papers in existence can be counted on the fingers of two hands. There are some interesting essay-exercises from a period of study in Brussels; some of her own drawings also survive [see Gérin, 1971]. These are highlights of what, compared with the surviving documents of many nineteenth- and twentieth-century writers, is a poor catch. Moreover, no close friends recording impressions of her at any length or in any intimacy have come to light. Despite fluctuations of feeling, her best friends *appear* to have been her family, but even her sisters did not leave the kind of record of Emily's life one might have expected, or even always wholly trustworthy impressions. The observations of former servants and the anecdotes of elderly Haworth residents enjoy a surprising prominence in Emily's biography.

The dangers of biography in Emily's case are many: reading too much out of surviving fragments of evidence; weighting them too heavily; filling in the gaps with wishful guesswork which reinforces presuppositions about Emily, and supposed contrasts with her sisters. There is the danger of trusting rumour and legend when other evidence is lacking, and of 'finding' thinly disguised autobiography at large in her novel and in her poetry. One can easily be tempted to see the lack of material as fairly reflecting a lack of event and activity in her life, or to see the enigma of that lack of material as reflecting some enigma in her personality. The image of a secretive, anti-social mystic, wrapped in and rapt by her visions, happier communing with animals and the moors than with people – whatever its degree of truth – has thrived within that very lack of evidence about her life, accentuated by uncertainty about her writing, and perhaps particularly about her poetry. She is the sphinx, the priestess. At times biography has simply played fast and loose with her. She has been attributed an illegitimate child (born, of course, on the moors), and the apparently urgent need to find her a lover (to explain her capacity to portray the passion of Heathcliff and Cathy) has resulted in their being conveniently 'found' in her clergyman-father's curates, in any male figure in her poetry, in any neighbouring lad of an appropriate age, and even in the title of one of her manuscript poems, misread as a man's name. She has been diagnosed as having been in love with her sister Anne, with her father, with her brother – most recently with her dead sister Maria. Even the judicious Spark and Stanford show unjustified assurance in talking about Emily's 'unbalanced mind' [p. 87]. Biography abhors a vacuum, and with so little to restrain them, all sorts and conditions of one-legged theories have hopped onto the stage. In consequence, what can be said with any confidence about Emily's life and mind must often, as in Chitham's study, be rigorously phrased in terms of degrees of probability and be the consequence of inference, perhaps at a number of removes, from shards of evidence concerning not just Emily, but her whole family.

Yet here is another problem, for Emily, Charlotte and Anne have also tended to be seen as manifestations of a composite known as '*The* Brontës', which at times would extend to include their father, their brother Branwell, and at its most speculative even their eldest sisters, Maria and Elizabeth, who died in childhood. It is an approach with much attraction and some justification. The idea of a tightly knit group of children, differentiated in character but closely of an age (and the more close emotionally for the death of their mother), interacting in both their domestic and imaginative lives as they grew up, and doing so for the most part in the unluxurious environment of the Haworth Parsonage on the Yorkshire Moors, is magnetically appealing. That appeal has been almost independent of the children's subsequent adult writing, the 'Brontës' phenomenon offering itself as a rich contribution to the mythography of childhood.

Moreover, each child certainly did nurture the imaginative life and literary energies of the others in games, in songs, in poems, in romances and eventually in novels. In pairs (Charlotte and Branwell, Anne and Emily), the children wrote and illustrated literary works of their own, developing out of their early games with toy soldiers the heroic figures and events of ever-extendible imaginary lands called Angria and Gondal. Out of this communal activity there eventually came not just *Wuthering Heights* but *Jane Eyre* and *The Tenant of Wildfell Hall*, thereby allowing that whole childhood culture also to be approached as a case-study in the chemistry of the literary imagination. If ever the elusive conditions of creativity were accidentally – magically – brought together into a force-field affecting all within its influence, it has often seemed that it was within the stones of Haworth Parsonage, itself so evocatively backing onto a ready-made image of romantic afflatus in the wild and windswept moors themselves. So, if fascination with the Brontës has partly centred on them in the plural, biography of each in the singular has implicitly had to live with suspicions of being doomed to the condition of a fragment of some greater key. Vatic theories of literary production and acceptance of the phenomenon of 'the Brontës' have tended to reinforce each other: they were all 'eagles'. In consequence, the just biographer of a Brontë in the singular, and Emily in particular, has had to follow an uncertain path in itself and to negotiate between minimal traces of the subject and the seductive appeal of large-scale 'Brontës' myths standing ready and extremely willing to supply gaps and organise the structure of what is often essentially and simply unknown – or, at least, a percentage game of probabilities.

When reading biographical accounts of Emily, Muriel Spark and Derek Stanford emphasised, it is crucial to distinguish between versions utilising sources stemming from her lifetime, and those based on statements made after Emily's death, when a snowball of mythicisation was already rolling. For the latter process Charlotte bears a heavy responsibility [see Drew; Grove, 1986]. The sister with the sharpest appreciation of the contemporary economic and cultural conditions of publishing, it was she – initially against Emily's wishes – who prompted the publication of the sisters' poetry in 1846, and who, after Emily's death, gave the public their first representation of the author of *Wuthering Heights*. The authority of Charlotte's view of Emily naturally imposed itself in a situation where many readers had not previously been sure even of Ellis Bell's sex; today's readers may still not realise how much their view of Emily, and of her novel, has been determined by Charlotte's biographical and critical legacy as 'proprietress of their reputations' [Brick, 1960, p. 356].

In her 'Biographical Notice of Ellis and Acton Bell' (pp. 359–65) Charlotte deferred rather more than in her fiction to society's dominant values. In writing of the sisters' early dream of becoming 'authors', she used the term to denote a public and professional status. (In the literal sense they had been authors from their earliest years.) Charlotte wrote of herself and her sisters from the viewpoint of that world of authorship and publishing to which she (who dedicated the second edition of *Jane Eyre* to Thackeray) particularly aspired. (Emily may well have suspected that world of being full of Lockwoods.) The values of the audience Charlotte addressed in her 'Biographical Notice' were male and clubbish in tone; Emily's poems could be recommended as being not 'at all like the poetry women generally write' – although later, trapped in double negatives, Charlotte found herself wanting to assert the conventionally 'feminine' in the sisters' writings. That audience's values were also metropolitan, and here her concession was to describe herself and her sisters as being 'resident in a remote district'. Remote from where, one might ask? Haworth? Halifax? Yorkshire? Liverpool? The North of England? The Industrial Revolution? Remote, one must conclude, from, and in the eyes of, London and a definitive metropolitan culture. This district was also one, says Charlotte, 'where education had made little progress'; and yet it had been sufficient to equip the Brontë sisters for their writing. Again, the comment defers to the educational institutions Charlotte associated with the culture she addressed, and the culture with which she herself identified at the expense of both Emily and Anne [*cf.* Grove, 1976, pp. 34–9]. There is, in short, a doubleness in Charlotte's mediation of Emily, Emily's writing and Emily's world: in stepping forward with news from that world, Charlotte steps out almost completely and reports on it with the adopted eyes of her audience. It is a strategy she used more self-consciously in her 'Editor's Preface' to *Wuthering Heights* (pp. 365–9), seeking to close the gap between the novel and the culture of the assumed reader, but perhaps actually widening it by so stressing the 'alien' and the 'unfamiliar' – not because the text featured, say, ghosts and exhumation, but because it represented Yorkshire rural life. Certainly Charlotte could simply assert the integrity of Emily's world as equal to that of the genteel metropolitan reader: 'her native hills were far more to her than a spectacle; they were what she lived in, and by'; but this was not her most characteristic tone.

Between the lines of the 'Biographical Notice' Emily emerges as someone – to Charlotte's irritation – who would not always do and think as Charlotte wished. Indeed, Charlotte's assessment, before the particular audience she addressed, of Emily's lack of 'worldly wisdom', Emily's unsuitedness to 'the practical business of life', Emily's failure 'to consult her most legitimate advantage', Emily's opposition of her inflexible 'will' to her 'interest', may well hint only at Emily's repeatedly not supporting Charlotte's schemes, or not doing what an older sister thought best. In context, Charlotte's influential epitome of Emily, 'an interpreter ought always to have stood between her and the world', is not a generous and admiring statement of Emily's pure unworldliness or a recognition of a cryptic mysticism, but an expression of some frustration, of apology, even of pity, towards a sister who resisted literary and domestic shaping. (During Emily's final illness Charlotte explained to a doctor that Emily would only do the opposite of what she was advised.) With heavy deference to a readership seen as culturally normative, the rather perverse Emily that Charlotte constructed was one whose judgement and intellect could hardly claim the audience's attention (being 'unripe', 'inefficiently cultured', 'partially expanded', with 'no thought of filling [her pitcher] at the well-spring of other minds'). What was left to promote in Emily was the originality of the primitive, her 'secret power and fire', the myth, as it was taken up, of 'a baby God'. In the 'Editor's Preface' Charlotte cast Emily as the sculptor who was but the tool of some greater power, the 'quiescent' channel working 'passively', the outcome in *Wuthering Heights* being 'half statue, half rock' – not wholly artistic, but naturally powerful, the product of the inspired rather than the conscious artist: 'She did not know what she had done.'

Aided by Mrs Gaskell, and by innumerable Victorian and Edwardian littérateurs, this is the version of Emily which has dominated the decades, and which has even made the search for detail of her life risk seeming irrelevant. Yet it is difficult to relate this Emily to the woman who crafted the narrative structure, inheritance plot, and detailed hidden chronology of *Wuthering Heights* [see Sanger]. Advances in recovering and understanding the position of women in the nineteenth century (of which Charlotte was elsewhere so conscious) have encouraged an attention to the typical in Emily's life and circumstances (as a woman of her class) as well as the unique [see Eagleton, 1975]. The challenging of metropolitan and elitist definitions of the norms of culture and lifestyle – the slow recognition that it may not necessarily have been gothically abnormal to have been young, female and to have lived in Yorkshire – has helped to humanise Emily and her world [Ewbank: Showalter]. That world itself is being increasingly recognised as nineteenth-century industrial England rather than some middle-earth of 'unbridled passions and simple earthy activities' [Cecil, p. 149].

Greater appreciation of her reading and of her access to local libraries erodes the image of the 'inefficiently cultured' writer [see Chitham and Winnifrith]; different ways of appreciating her family's Irish roots offer insights into the cultural tensions of the Brontës' place in English society of their time [Cannon]. Some of the insistently cryptic and 'mystical' elements of her poetry are being persuasively reinterpreted in ways which while weakening them as references to personal visionary experience, consolidate them as the meditations of a self-conscious writer who very often knew extremely well what she was doing [Chitham and Winnifrith, 1983]. The continuing need to exercise scepticism towards Charlotte's Emily, and the Emily of those enthusiasts who followed Charlotte's lead, goes hand-in-hand with the task of exercising caution towards the *Wuthering Heights* those lives have implied.

Sources: Perforations in Other Tanks

Charlotte Brontë, in stressing Emily's lack of direct contact with local Yorkshire people, nevertheless conceded that Emily 'knew them: knew their ways, their language, their family histories', and could 'talk of them with detail, minute, graphic and accurate'. For Charlotte, Emily had responded somewhat narrowly to the 'tragic and terrible' to be found in 'the secret annals of every rude vicinage', but she indicated that it was out of such material that Cathy and Heathcliff had been wrought (p. 366). The relationship of *Wuthering Heights* to folk culture and oral tradition has subsequently proved one element of a field of inquiry with implications not only for questions concerning Emily's originality, her experience, and her sense of herself as writer, but for the illumination of aspects of her novel's style, technique, themes, genre and unity. Some accounts of the novel [e.g. Q. D. Leavis] evaluate its strengths and weaknesses in terms of its capacity to harmonise such influences.

If only to dispose of it, the hypothesis most fundamentally affecting estimates of Emily's originality must be mentioned – the early laid claim that *Wuthering Heights* was partly or wholly written by her brother Branwell [see Anon; Willis]. This contention was always poorly substantiated and its traces are best viewed as a grotesque expression of that male Victorian mentality evident in many early reviews of the novel, which declined to recognise the language, depicted violence or passion of *Wuthering Heights* as the appropriate or possible products of a woman's pen – and certainly not for a female audience – while being quite content to assume the novel's power the product of a man's [see Ward, pp. 103–4; Nelson; Allott, 1974]. If a male author did not exist, then he had to be invented: Branwell – particularly as male solidarity required his rescuing from the shadow of three clever sisters – was splendidly convenient.

More rationally, three principal areas of interest have presented themselves: the relationship of *Wuthering Heights* to oral tradition, to pre-existing texts, and to Emily's own poetry.

Wuthering Heights itself recognises the vitality of an often superstitious oral tradition in the society it explores. Indeed the process whereby Lockwood is assumed to transcribe the largely unscripted narrative of Nelly Dean, the 'regular gossip' (p. 31), enacts historical transitions between oral and written narrative, emphasising the debt of the latter to the richness of the former. The narrating Nelly, although literate, displays an inheritance from those 'country folks' who repeat 'idle tales' about Heathcliff's ghost in just the way they and their forbears may be assumed to have mythicised community events for thousands of years (p. 336). Bell, in examining the novel 'as *Epos*' (i.e. as oral epic), argues that Nelly's narrative is 'meant to be heard, not read', and that it shares certain stylistic tendencies with the folk poetry of ballads: 'Nelly's sole responsibility is to the central action of her story; anything extraneous is cut away'; were Nelly writing rather than speaking, 'she would incur new responsibilities for detail indigenous to the novel'. Indeed, and chasteningly for many impressionistic accounts of the novel, Bell emphasises that except when Lockwood is directly observing, 'the novel is all but devoid of physical description' [p. 200] (and certainly so in comparison with the run of Victorian fiction [see Irwin]). Also like ballads, she contends, the novel is story-centred rather than character-centred. J. F. Goodridge [1976] has discussed the influence on *Wuthering Heights* of some particular ballads with a 'pre-Christian' pedigree [p. 171], and Edward Chitham [1987] shows ballads dealing with such ideas as a mourning lover being 'the cause of his sweetheart's inability to rest in the grave', and displaying, like Emily Brontë's novel, a sense of the dead simultaneously as 'decomposing body and as disembodied spirit' [p. 289]. Gose, also like Goodridge, emphasises the relevance of the fairy tale, another oral form, and one commonly concerned with the difficulties of growing up and the testing of pride and fidelity in the course of maturation.

The influence of oral tradition on Emily is supported by accounts of story-telling she heard from her father and from servants. Promoting the children's oral repetition of stories would appear to have been one of the Reverend Patrick Brontë's educational methods – and as such only an extension of familiar techniques in the transmission of culture. Exploration of the history of the Brontë family in Ireland has unearthed not only formidably accomplished individual story-tellers who may have contributed to Patrick's legacy of story-telling in terms of stock and technique (including a high colouring of Celtic gothic with an inbuilt rhetoric and dramatis personae of fairies, ghosts and demons), but also particular family stories with a bearing on *Wuthering Heights* [Cannon; Chitham, 1987]. Most notable is the story of 'Welsh' Prunty (Brontë), which in dealing with the theme of the outsider who achieves power within the family, persuasively stands as an anticipation of aspects of Heathcliff, his situation and actions. Similar themes have also been traced in the oral and written history attaching to Yorkshire country houses near which Emily briefly lived [Simpson; Chitham, 1987]. Being persuaded that such stories did help shape Heathcliff and *Wuthering Heights* does more than satisfy curiosity: it can affect an understanding, through the nature of such sources, of what might otherwise appear the gratuitously melodramatic property-plot of the novel. Family history, in its concern for the particular family as value, can hardly regard such tales of the outsider-made-insider as just entertainment, but as sites where the nature, continuity and responsibilities of the family itself are crucially investigated, tested, adapted and resolved, in a way necessarily significant to every family member and each passing generation in the continuing story of the family. The story of Welsh Prunty came to Emily in such terms; it would hardly be surprising if her reworking of its themes in *Wuthering Heights* maintained a nucleus of similar concerns.

Discussion of relationships between Emily's writing and pre-existing texts has also been important in enlarging assessments of the scale of literary experience she brought to her writing, in objectifying the mix of literary tone and ideas to which she was exposed – and in curbing more eccentric explanations of textual features of her novel [see Blondel]. Her father's library at Haworth was that of a poet as well as of a clergyman, and opportunities to extend the range of her reading were offered by the Keighley Mechanics' Institute Library and that of a neighbouring country house, Ponden Hall. Nevertheless, Emily was still a clergyman's daughter: while she does not allude to the Bible as freely as Charlotte, Shannon interestingly highlights her use in Jabes Branderham's sermon of Peter's question to Christ concerning the number of times he should forgive his brother, and Christ's reply, 'Until seventy times seven'. Shannon sees Lockwood's and Branderham's mutual accusations of having committed a sin one beyond the seventy times seven as a proposition within the novel of the possibility of an unpardonable sin, which Shannon identifies with Cathy's marrying Edgar rather than Heathcliff. (Other commentators suggest a gamut of unpardonable sins, from lack of mercy to abandoning children.) Interpretations such as Miller's [1963] and Davies's, however, assume such an allusion to be only the tip of an iceberg of Biblical awareness.

Sir Walter Scott's fiction has long been regarded as a significant general influence, both in terms of its moorland settings and its romantic tenor, and there have been various attempts to pin down a particular indebtedness on Emily's part to such of Scott's novels as *The Heart of Midlothian, Old Mortality, The Black Dwarf* [Dry; Goodridge, 1976], *Redgauntlet* [Holloway], and *Waverley* [Jack], as to Hogg's *Confessions of a Justified Sinner* [Hewish]. Bartholomew Simmonds's story 'The Bridegroom of Barna', which appeared in *Blackwood's Magazine* for November 1840 – a journal known to have been 'staple reading' [Gérin, 1966, p. 1] in the Brontë household – has proved a rather more convincing instance of particular indebtedness. In particular, it contains a scene in which, as Bradner and MacKay point out, the hero, an Irishman, disinters the body of the girl he loves: 'enclosing in his arms the form that had once comprised all earth's love and beauty for him. . . . The wan face was turned up to his as if it could still thrill to the mad kisses in which he steeped it, while he had twined one of the white arms around his neck' [MacKay, p. 33]. MacKay explores possible connections between this story and *Wuthering Heights* in detail, and also between the novel and a German story of property and revenge, Hoffmann's *Das Majorat* (also previously highlighted by Wilson), arguing that these contrasting sources contribute to the peculiar tensions of *Wuthering Heights*: 'the world of primary passions is the world of the Irish tale, and the world of conscious propriety is the world of the German tale' [p. 29]. This kind of perspective has implicitly lent support to interpretations constructed around conflict between a world of primitive, natural passion in Wuthering Heights, and the 'civilised decadence' [Traversi, p. 170] of Thrushcross Grange.

As long ago as 1857 John Skelton noted the 'genuine

reminiscence' [*cit.* Allott, 1970, p. 74] of Ophelia's madness in Cathy's delirium, while the eponymous villain-heroes of *Macbeth* and *Richard III* have often been mooted as shadowing the creation of Heathcliff. Girdler notes quotation from *Twelfth Night* and an allusion to *King Lear*, explores other verbal echoes of Shakespeare's plays, and most notably, like Leslie Stephen [*cit.* Allott, 1970, p. 100], suggests a model for Heathcliff's actions in the strategies of the Renaissance Revengers, including Hamlet. Certainly there at times seem hints of Websterian grotesquerie in Heathcliff's language; moreover, Heathcliff's unquestioning extension of his revenge beyond Hindley and Edgar into persecution of Hareton and Catherine is more recognisable when understood in relation to versions of vendetta.

More attuned to comparisons in terms of sureness of feeling and language, and maturity of apprehension of humanity's place in the universe, Klingopulos moves frequently between the novel and Elizabethan drama to propose *Wuthering Heights* as the first English novel to aim at a seriousness comparable to that of such drama, understood – with Greek drama – as a universal touchstone of value and achievement. Collins wrote similarly of the Lear element in the novel, finding an Elizabethan influence in the language 'so completely absorbed that there remains no direct reminiscence to be observed' [p. 47]. Vincent Buckley and Ingeborg Nixon, like Klingopulos, have seen the novel as being structured by the language of certain great speeches, and so see the text revealing its debt, within its larger 'fusion of elements' [Buckley, p. 5], to the same body of drama.

Gothic fiction in general has been examined for influence, though with an awareness of marked differences between the terms of Emily Brontë's interest in Gothic themes and that of eighteenth-century Gothic practitioners [see Blondel]; as Fenton put it, 'the supernatural in Emily Brontë is a *result*, not a *cause*' [p. 119]. Romantic poets – Byron, Keats, Shelley and Coleridge (the latter once complaining of the tendency of critics to see new work only as 'perforations in other men's tanks') – clearly influenced Emily strongly. (As for Wordsworth, he was actually sent a copy of the 1846 *Poems*. Perceived similarities between the visionary-revolutionary in Blake and Emily Brontë have notably fuelled feminist arguments of the last ten years – counterpointed by vigorous disagreement over her view of Milton [Gilbert and Gubar; Davies].) The presence of Byron, and such of his heroes as Cain and Manfred, has been well traced in the Brontës' juvenilia: Winifred Gérin [1966] attributes some of the typical figures in Emily's fantasy world of Gondal (outlaws, bandits, exiles and prisoners) to models provided by Byron. Ann Lapraik Livermore argues that *Wuthering Heights* contains features of Byron's poem 'The Dream' and that it also picks up elements of story and detail from Byron's own life. Byron's persona, and his dark moody heroes, passionate, proud, rebellious, sinning and exiled, prompt Gérin, summing up what many have thought, to describe Heathcliff as the most Byronic figure in all literature. However, as Arnold Kettle points out, Heathcliff does not spring entirely from the pages of Byron.

Of recent work the most stimulating has arguably been Edward Chitham's investigations of Shelley's influence [1983]. The poet who wrote 'Epipsychidion', addressed to Emilia Viviani, a poem embodying a concept of love as a fusion of souls, might well be understood to have had a special place in the affections and imagination of another Emily who could also regard herself as being addressed by the poet. Chitham finds Emily not only influenced in style, and learning from Shelley's Neo-Platonism ways of framing ideas about transcendence through love, but sees Shelley himself personally portrayed in her poetry as spirit-hero and poetic mentor. Moreover, contrary to the common supposition that in reading romantic poets Emily 'had no interest in the political aspects of . . . Liberty' [Cooper, p. 107], he also posits her movement not so much towards paganism as towards a non-Christian Shelleyan radicalism by the time she wrote *Wuthering Heights*.

As evidence of the influence of other writers' works has accumulated, so also has there developed appreciation of the novel's incubation in Emily's poetry of the 1830s and early 1840s. To expect relationships between her poetry and her novel is only reasonable (Charles Morgan termed them 'twins of a unique imagination' [*cit*. Hatfield, p. 11]), yet there have proved pitfalls even in clearing the ground for exploration.

Relatively few of Emily's poems were published in her lifetime. Charlotte, as meddling editor, changed and even augmented some of those which she saw through the press after Emily's death. Some became entangled through transcription by other hands with poems by Charlotte, Branwell and Anne, resulting in temporary errors of attribution – a danger increased by the similarity of the Brontë children's special miniature scripts. Despite Emily's apparent intention to separate her poetry into different notebooks, there has been room for disagreement about which poems deal with the fantasy land of Gondal she shared in play, prose and poetry with Anne, and which can be described as non-Gondal – disagreement about which are essentially dramatic and which essentially lyrical [see Bradner]. The hope that a fully consistent version of the world of Gondal is recoverable from the poems has led to optimistically over-developed theories seeking to reconstruct that world (sometimes assuming, such as Ratchford's, that *all* the poems are Gondal poems). Such theories always run the risk of imposing closure on what was undoubtedly an open-ended activity. Like the apprenticeship in imagination of Auden and Isherwood's fantasy worlds, Gondal is best understood as a stream of characteristic images, situations and themes rather than a complete artefact, or even a fragment of one. It was for Anne and Emily a means of conversing, of thinking, of symbolising and of writing, something to slide into and out of, rather than a systematically achieved or even envisaged end. If the sisters were able to write prose 'histories' of their imaginary land, it was not because its history was fixed in brass, but because their own exclusive possession of Gondal gave them alone the right to be its historians, and to arrogate to themselves the delectable authority they found displayed in the writings of historians of more tangible lands. Gondal freed them into writing, perhaps particularly as children, and again, as female writers [*cf.* Senf].

When the poetry is read intertextually with *Wuthering Heights*, continuities of language, image, character, situation and theme are readily evident. It is hard to read 'Cold in the Earth' with its faithful heroine thinking of her lover's grave and of her faithfulness to him through the fifteen years since his death, and not to think of Heathcliff's love for the dead Cathy: 'Faithful indeed is the spirit that remembers / After such years of change and suffering!' [Hatfield, p. 223]. It is hard to read 'No Coward Soul is Mine' [Hatfield, pp. 242–3] and not find a version of Cathy's statement of the intensity of her love for Heathcliff. And it is equally hard not to find, as Bradner and Van Ghent do, some version of Cathy and Heathcliff (or, like Visick, of Catherine and Hareton) in the two poems Charlotte Brontë dubbed 'The Two Children', where a 'Child of Delight with sunbright hair' befriends a 'mournful boy', swearing 'to take his gloomy sadness / And give to him my beamy joy': 'Fate is strong, but Love is stronger; / And more unsleeping than angel's care' [Hatfield, p. 230]. Hatfield also points out the similarity between Cathy's sentiments concerning Heaven and Emily's lines [p. 12]:

> We would not leave our native home
> For *any* world beyond the Tomb.
> No – rather on thy kindly breast
> Let us be laid in lasting rest;
> Or waken but to share with thee
> A mutual immortality.

Throughout her predominantly melancholy poetry so often dealing with exclusion and separation, the intervention of death between lovers is a recurrent theme, as also, however, is the role of the body as the prison-house of the soul – leading to flashes where transcendence and union are intuited. Whether lyrical or dramatic, the poetry explored versions of the ideas of *Wuthering Heights* long before the novel was contemplated. As Traversi and Miller [1963] argued, there is a quasi-religious intensity about Cathy and Heathcliff's love, and its roots lie in the poetry.

Socially realised only in stylised ways, the characters of Emily's fantasy world inevitably express their dilemmas principally through natural and elemental imagery (though also through a heroic furniture of ships and dungeons, castles and battles). This tendency persisted when she exchanged Gondal for a historical Yorkshire with which her own life was continuous. Some readers – particularly those who insist on Emily as poet rather than as novelist – consequently approach Gondal as 'Heathcliff's Country' [Dodds], and treat the Yorkshire of *Wuthering Heights* as just another Gondal, an enabling setting which serves to frame characters in collision only with the eternal forces of a fantasy land. Yet however much *Wuthering Heights* owes its gestation to Gondal – and it owes much – it also has other allegiances. Joseph counting out on his Bible the day's takings, Heathcliff shutting up the Heights against the snow, Nelly and Zillah's brisk professional relationship – all these (to employ a term Emily used in her poetry to describe imagination) owe little to the 'phantom bliss' [Hatfield, p. 206] of Gondal. While *Wuthering Heights* has its sources and its influences, it moves beyond them. Charting those influences has produced valuable insights; but perhaps we would read the novel less if the known explained it more.

Narrative: the Villain in the Chinese Box

The distinctive narrative structure of *Wuthering Heights*, so dependent on Lockwood and Nelly Dean, has long attracted comment and not always admiration.

Dobell, in 1850, while writing appreciatively of the novel, hoped that in future the author would avoid using a 'housekeeper who remembers two volumes *literatim*' [*cit.* Allott, 1970, p. 61]. Swinburne, although favourably disposed, found the book's construction difficult and awkward; Garrod spoke of 'inferior technique' and of it being 'in general ill constructed' [*cit.* Allott, 1970, p. 134]. Van Ghent, however, found it 'highly wrought' [p. 187] and memorably described the narrative structure as a set of Chinese boxes, each inside the next. Her description remains extremely apt, especially in capturing such an extended convolution as the reader encountering Emily Brontë's text reporting Lockwood writing for himself, or for his friends, an account of Nelly Dean's report of Isabella's letter giving Joseph's report of what Heathcliff was saying downstairs. Gleckner, stressing how the novel renders past time while commencing in 1801 and ending in 1802, sees the achievement of the narrative technique in its conveying, 'without using stream of consciousness, a kind of all-pervading present, of which the past and future are integral parts' [p. 330]. Certainly the narrative technique produces an intensely dramatic form, self-enclosed, free of moralising authorial commentary, and in its relativity of narration arguably imbued with a 'radical uncertainty' about its own interpretation [Holderness, p. 5].

Serious discussion of the artistry of novels having gained a specific impetus from the novelist Henry James's theory and practice in the use of point of view and from subsequent studies of the mediation of stories, the narratorial roles of Nelly and Lockwood inevitably stimulated further scrutiny, and indeed enhanced valuations. Jacobs has recently provided a striking riposte to the earliest opinions in observing that in relation to their main stories, 'the Brontës' framing narratives are more like competing works of art, or outer rooms in a gallery, or even the picture painted over a devalued older canvas' [p. 207].

Critics found that narrators showed tendencies, like Chaucer's pilgrims, to jump into the focus of their respective stories' concerns. Marlow was not just Conrad's shadowy story-teller, but a characterised human sounding-board, deeply implicated in the tales he narrated; Nick Carraway was not just a neutral viewpoint but a centre of the moral and emotional tensions of *The Great Gatsby*. Certain narrators, such as Defoe's Moll Flanders, have become the centre of critical debates enjoying an almost classic status in English studies. Although some observers have been happy to continue speaking of Nelly as 'the author's authority in the novel', of the 'trustworthiness of the narrator' [Buckler, pp. 54–5] – and even of her being 'steady as an oil-tanker in dirty weather' [Bloomfield, p. 304] – Nelly has also been isolated for investigation as an unreliable narrator whose judgements have to be viewed sceptically.

Nelly is narrator, character and actor [*cf.* Langman]. She is a character, in that she is related in highly specific social and personal ways to those around her, and in possessing a marked and complex personality. She is an actor in that she is a great deal more than a fly on the wall in relation to the story. She is physically present at many key moments, advising and reproving, passing judgements at the time and with hindsight, taking action on her own initiative, expressing allegiances, effectively working to promote or prevent particular occurrences.

Part of any writer's task in using such a narrator lies in ensuring the credibility of their witnessing events. This can sometimes be achieved by such expedients as conveniently allowing doors to be left open, but the requirement that narrators be present at certain scenes can, notoriously, force them as characters into unlikely, even perilous situations. Arguably for her pains in the service of narrative, Nelly is herself at various times threatened with a knife by Hindley, not to mention being kidnapped and roughly handled by Heathcliff. Bounds are observed in *Wuthering Heights*: it would not be credible for Nelly to witness Cathy and Edgar's bedroom conversations or Heathcliff's graveyard activities – Cathy and Heathcliff must confide such information to Nelly. Yet to make such a qualification is to acknowledge implications for the characterisation of Cathy and Heathcliff: however their separate relationships with Nelly might have fallen out under the conditions of a different narrative technique, they must under these conditions be presented as habitually willing to entrust Nelly with such confidences. In the writing of *Wuthering Heights* narrative technique clearly interacted with character and event, each importantly modifying the other, although, from the evidence of the text alone, the exact relationship of chicken and egg may not be recoverable. Even if one senses that, say, Isabella's writing to Nelly is unlikely [Watson, 1949b], or that Heathcliff's perennial willingness to reveal his feelings, actions and plans to Nelly is principally dictated by the technical needs of composition [Edgar], the dramatic implications of their willingness to do so have still to be reckoned with. The narrative technique, then, is by no means just the scaffolding enabling the edifice to be built; it is the interior steel reinforcing which contributes to the form of the whole.

Hafley took the matter of Nelly's involvement in events to the extreme conclusion in 'The Villain in *Wuthering Heights*'. Writing against a consensus view of Nelly as, in Charlotte Brontë's words, 'a specimen of true benevolence and homely fidelity' (p. 367), Hafley preferred to stress such minority interpretations as Pritchett's, which painted Nelly as 'an obdurate architect of the tragedy' [*cit*. Hafley, p. 200]. (Pritchett based this on Nelly's not revealing Heathcliff's presence during the conversation with Cathy which crucially provokes Heathcliff's leaving the Heights.) Many other critics have stressed Nelly's ordinariness: Nelly's telling the story thereby places it within the realm of 'the psychologically familiar' [Van Ghent, p. 189], or constitutes a simple foil to the extraordinariness of her story and its characters, the housekeeper standing – with Lockwood – as the 'pedestrian spectator, whose imperceptive evaluations serve to understate the demonic passion and feeling in the novel' [Reynolds, p. 31].

Hafley, however, offers grounds for seeing Nelly as a wilful, manipulative character motivated by a 'romantic dream for herself' [p. 204] and by a greed and an ambition finding expression in her mercenary allegiance to the Lintons as a family, and in the 'mean success' [p. 214] of her steady promotion through the novel. For Hafley, these priorities on her part issue in morally dubious behaviour towards her masters and towards Heathcliff and Cathy. Indeed, disasters which she might easily have prevented are precipitated through Nelly. Meier subsequently observed that Nelly is 'not merely a catalyst but an agent in the destruction of Cathy and the fall of Edgar' [p. 234].

While there are holes to be picked in some of Hafley's points, his argument is strengthened by the charges Cathy makes, 'Nelly, *you* have helped to unsettle me! . . . Ah! Nelly has played traitor . . . Nelly is my hidden enemy – you witch!' (pp. 125, 129), and by some of Nelly's own reflections:

> I seated myself in a chair, and rocked, to and fro, passing harsh judgment on my many derelictions of duty; from which, it struck me then, all the misfortunes of all my employers sprang. It was not the case, in reality, I am aware; but it was, in my imagination, that dismal night; and I thought Heathcliff himself less guilty than I. (p. 277)

'Well,' says Nelly to Lockwood with disarming frankness at one point, 'we *must* be for ourselves in the long run' (p. 92).

Nelly's prejudices, her moral compromises and equivocations, suppressions of information, betrayals of trust, role-playings and deceptions, are certainly there in the text to confound more trusting views of her benevolence. However, the problematical in Nelly may partly stem from the author's technical problem of repeatedly having to allow Nelly into the confidence of all sides in the novel's conflicts in order for her to narrate events. That being so, the author also has to prevent her short-circuiting matters by some splendidly moral or committedly local intervention. In short, Nelly's formal function as narrator may have determined her problematical character. This accepted, the housekeeper's fleeting consideration and rejection of her own culpability for events need not be read as an ironic indictment of Nelly, but as Emily Brontë's recognition of this whole side-effect of the narrative technique and as her attempt to bounce the reader out of just such a harsh judgement of Nelly. Woodring observes Emily Brontë scrupulously attempting to prevent 'Nelly's actions from seeming to modify in any way either the personalities of the more important characters or the major directions of the plot' [p. 303]. Nevertheless, if the author did make such an attempt, the text also suggests she was not entirely successful.

Determined to present Nelly as the complete villain, Hafley overstated his case. Nelly is no conscious schemer of the Iago school, neither are her actions quite so crucial as Hafley suggests. Building on Hafley's evidence, however, Kenney developed the argument into an exploration of the unconscious Nelly who once hoped to marry Hindley. Her low opinion of Frances as Hindley's wife is thus explained by jealousy. Without Hindley, Nelly is left a frustrated admirer of unobtainable men (and particularly gentlemen), in general unimpressed by women, and further venting her frustration in a particular lack of sympathy towards Cathy and such of the girl's problems as are generated by the ease with which – in contrast to Nelly – she arouses the interest of men. Nelly's commitment to '*my* Hareton', the Hareton she has 'mothered' as nurse, is an extension of her commitment to the Hindley she never won and the child of his that she never bore. In Kenney's view, 'she is to find contentment only in the maternal role, not in the romantic one' [p. 230]: sexual psychology, then, rather than conscious power-seeking, underlies Nelly's more problematical actions and stances.

Nelly's 'villainy' will hardly bear regarding as a conscious scheming; it emerges in her responding to situations as they occur with a certain officiousness, self-interest and amour-propre, and with a desire always to avoid in the short term the kinds of trouble, embarrassment and disruptions of the status quo which she is puzzled to find that more passionate people seem intent on causing [*cf*. Mathison]. Care for the short term, however, as when she accompanies Catherine to the Heights, often only creates paradox in the long term.

Critics such as Gilbert and Gubar, and Kavanagh, have more recently shifted the problem of Nelly's conduct from the ground of moral villainy, through emotional disappointment or sexual neurosis, to the broader issue of her ideological stance, highlighting, as Kettle did many years ago, that very commonsense with which Nelly has so often been approvingly credited by critics (as by Lockwood). In this perspective hers is a conventional commonsense exhibiting absorption of the values of the system she serves, that same system which in turn oppresses Cathy and Heathcliff. The qualities which Charlotte Brontë saw may well be there, but they are highly ambiguous characteristics which holographically change appearance according to the angle from which they are viewed. While Nelly identifies herself and her interests with a family by which she is only employed (the Lintons), she hardly ever mentions her own real family: she has surrendered the Deans in the Earnshaws and the Lintons, as she often surrenders the claims of women (and particularly Cathy) to the authority of men. For Gilbert and Gubar she is 'patriarchy's paradigmatic housekeeper' [p. 291]. As I shall develop the point in my 'Appraisal', Nelly is perhaps at worst an ideological drifter who fails, despite occasional insights and acts of sympathy towards the young Heathcliff, fully to see a reflection of the real foundations of her own condition in terms of class and gender, as servant and woman, in either Heathcliff or in Cathy. She picks up her short-term comforts and small but gratifying rewards from a society she unreflectingly shores up and which she chooses to live *with* rather than against. It is hardly villainy. It is perhaps the consent and the contradiction, the conscious and unconscious complicity, which any hierarchical system of power requires of the middle rank to maintain its own stability: in short, Nelly's complicity – as 'mistress of the double-bind' [A. Smith, p. 24] – disturbingly resembles the conformist face of the reader.

Writing / Erasing / Reading Sexuality

The achievement of *Wuthering Heights* as a novel about passion has often been presented as standing in inverse ratio to its supposedly minimal concern with sexuality. Moser, indeed, highlights 'the evident comfort that enthusiasts take in the notion that Cathy and Heathcliff's love is "sexless", meaning, presumably, that intercourse is not even implied' [p. 3]. Certainly the text's account of their love offers little by way of the repertory of physical human tenderness beyond snatched kisses and embraces – most of these concentrated into one scene. It is a short step to seeing the relationship as one which not only dwarfs physical sexual relations but which, as a 'sexless, consubstantial affinity' [Willson, p. 23], does not by nature express itself through them [Ford].

Discounting Cathy and Heathcliff as sexual beings, however, has sometimes been the accompaniment to sentimentality (promoting the novel as a morally 'acceptable' classic for children). It has also been a feature of the most colourful strand in the skein of Emily Brontë criticism, those symbolic and mystical interpretations which literalise Emily Brontë's metaphors and cast the characters as embodiments of amoral cosmic forces [Cecil; Van Ghent], or as exponents in an allegory of a mystical / Platonic union of souls.

Conviction of what Cecil terms the novel's moral unorthodoxy in, for example, positioning the reader to sympathise with a Heathcliff simultaneously understood as 'the greatest villain in fiction' [*cit.* Allott, 1970, p. 88], and with a Cathy who is – sexless or not – an adulteress, may well have played a part in the critical recasting of *Wuthering Heights* as cosmic myth. Such interpretations tend to reduce the pressure to confront that 'moral unorthodoxy' and its implications. The moralistic nineteenth-century reviewer detecting such unorthodoxy slammed the book down, roundly damned it as a 'pesthouse' and, by way of critical judgement, offered the injunction 'burn *Wuthering Heights*' [*cit.* Allott, 1970, p. 50]. Burning the novel sacrifices its power along with its moral unorthodoxy; but Heathcliff's violence and Cathy's rebelliousness are far less disturbing to the moral censor when understood as tending towards 'vibrations in the primordial surge of things' [Van Ghent, p. 193] – as opposed to actions and desires of man and woman in society. If Heathcliff 'is no more ethically relevant than is flood or earthquake or whirlwind' [Van Ghent, p. 201], the problematic in, say, his striking a young girl in the face is deflected or disguised. In short, while making considerable contributions to the appreciation of the figurative complexity of the text, such interpretations have run the risk of erasing Cathy and Heathcliff as images of humanity. Against these tendencies, Langman speaks of the dangers of dissolving the novel in 'a universal solvent of mythopoeic criticism' [p. 295], while Moody emphasises the novel's 'intense attachment to *this* world' [p. 29]. Rossetti perhaps captured this whole problem of the text's 'socio-metaphysical realism' [Buckley, p. 5], its awareness of human morality in society as well as of eschatology, in observing that 'the action is laid in Hell, – only it seems places and people have English names there' [*cit*. Allott, 1970, p. 71.] However, if one thought arising from Rossetti's quip might be that perhaps Hell *is* England, much discussion has chosen to operate in realms which do not even favour the framing of such an issue.

To slip from a view of Cathy and Heathcliff's relationship as 'sexless' to next speaking of it as *transcending* sexuality begs the question of whether such a term is appropriate to describe not so much a passing through, as what would be an evasion or bypassing of the 'transcended'. Indeed, to the extent that such a lack of sexuality is interpretable as a mark of immaturity in human terms, the relationship has variously been described (although not necessarily pejoratively) as childlike, adolescent [Federico], characteristic of first love. Moody, redeploying T. S. Eliot's words on *Hamlet*, offers it as the product of feelings uniquely experienced in adolescence, '"an intense feeling, ecstatic or terrible . . . exceeding its object", which Emily Brontë kept alive for herself and in her novel by her "ability to intensify the world to her emotions"' [p. 30]. Alternatively, seeing resemblances between Cathy and Heathcliff's relationship and that of a brother and sister, some observers have seen the protagonists as effectively trapped by the operation of an incest-taboo on sexual relationship evolving dramatically as a felt constraint out of Heathcliff's assumption of the role of son, and thus of Cathy's brother, within the Earnshaw family [Goetz]; or, somewhat wildly, as a consequence of Heathcliff's actually being Earnshaw's illegitimate son and thus literally Cathy's half-brother [Solomon]. (Hence also the formulation of biographical/psychoanalytical speculations about Emily's feelings towards her own brother Branwell.)

Wion proposes the relationship as 'a displaced version of the symbiotic relationship between mother and child' [p. 146], signalled, as Kovel also notes, by the rapid disappearance of mothers from the novel (Mrs Earnshaw, Mrs Linton, Frances,

Cathy, Isabella) and the prominence (especially in connection with Heathcliff) of an oral imagery (teeth, mouths, biting, gnashing) which, in Freudian terms, speaks of an arrested infantile development, and which is seen as ultimately deriving from Emily's premature loss of her mother.

Some observers have started quite cheerfully from the premise that there is nothing at all of human experience in the relationship: 'the relationship is of an ideal nature; it does not exist in life' [Collins, p. 43]. Clearly, if it is to be seen as sexual at all, the heated and largely unsated intensity of Cathy and Heathcliff's passion must at least be acknowledged as patterning a one-sided experience of sexuality as a process of extended anticipation riddled with some necessity of its own frustration – what one might term a principle of perpetually procrastinated sexual closure.

So what can be said about the presence of sexuality in the novel? Children are born into it (and the dates of their conception may even be calculated [Moser]); Cathy and Heathcliff themselves become parents; it is quite clear in the novel when Cathy and Heathcliff are each, separately, passing through puberty. Yet these factors have not prevented readers intuiting, or insisting upon, a disjunction between the novel's acknowledgement of sexuality in human relationships, indirectly evidenced in such ways, and the more sublime and chaste emotions which are understood to drive and unite hero and heroine (who would, simultaneously, be unthinkable as anything other than sexually attractive.)

Certainly those relationships in the novel in which sexual activity can be logically deduced hardly enjoy any automatic superiority to Cathy and Heathcliff's: the relationships of Mr and Mrs Earnshaw, or of Mr and Mrs Linton, do not compete with the protagonists' in passionate feeling. Moreover, while active sexual enjoyment plays a significant part in Hindley and Frances's relationship, their sexual play, with Frances on Hindley's knee, 'kissing and talking nonsense by the hour', is pointedly scorned by Cathy in her diary as 'foolish palaver' of which she and Heathcliff would be 'ashamed' (p. 19). This is recognisably a child's comment, but also not inconsistent with the visible terms of Cathy and Heathcliff's later relationship. Also, one may well detect in Frances's death in childbirth (the consumptive 'rush of a lass' (p. 63) given to hysterical emotion), despite Nelly's contempt and Kenneth's sangfroid, a pointed reflection upon woman as front-line physical victim of human sexuality. (Cathy's own death following childbirth reinforces the point.)

Certainly a deeply worrying idea of the husband and sexuality is available in the depiction of Linton. While Nelly's revulsion from the very idea of his marrying Catherine hinges upon Linton's physical ineffectiveness (as well as concern about property implications), the awfulness of the prospect lies in the distasteful certainty, notwithstanding, of the sexual rights marriage will conventionally and legally accord this 'perishing monkey' over a 'healthy, hearty girl' (p. 272) – merely on the strength of the monkey being male.

As it happens, Linton's sensual appetite is less focused on Catherine than on the sticks of sugar-candy he self-regardingly sucks. However, his complicity in Heathcliff's imprisonment of Catherine in the marriage bedroom (where Heathcliff, at least, plans consummation to occur), is extremely disturbing. An idea of the explicit and implicit violence of the situation manufactured in that bedroom – whatever Catherine may feel for Linton – is available in his cruel physical image voyeuristically capturing the effects of Heathcliff's striking Catherine:

> I wink to see my father strike a dog, or a horse, he does it so hard – yet I was glad at first – she deserved punishing for pushing me: but when papa was gone, she made me come to the window and showed me her cheek cut on the inside, against her teeth, and her mouth filling with blood . . . I sometimes think she can't speak for pain. (p. 281)

Hierarchies of power, of which the cowardly Linton is always acutely aware, are here brought into play and the dominating actions of this older Heathcliff located within them: human/animal; father/son; male/female. The blow is a deflowering of Catherine displaced into a discourse of power, violence and punishment, significantly performed by Heathcliff as the incapable Linton's proxy as he simultaneously and symbolically asserts the ascendancy of Linton's new rights as husband by crushing underfoot the locket-portrait of Catherine's father. The image of the wound resonates with what Gilbert and Gubar interpret as the phallic wounding of Cathy by the dogs at Thrushcross Grange: 'his huge, purple tongue hanging half a foot out of his mouth, and his pendant lips streaming with bloody slaver' (p. 47). It also resonates with the widowed Hindley, drunk and angrily frustrated, not only assaulting Nelly but enacting a displaced attempt at rape in demanding she open her mouth, and in then pushing the point of a carving knife between her teeth. Kenney speaks of the 'shape metaphor' in this episode, and, in key with the complexity of Nelly's character and her cool and blackly humorous handling of these events, sees Nelly here as an 'almost willing . . . recipient of male violence' [p. 227]. (Analogously, Moser sees Hindley's frustrated state figured in Nelly's prior action of taking 'the shot out of the master's fowling piece' [p. 9].)

As so often in nineteenth-century writing, it is not that sexuality is absent, but that its availability in the text is not restricted to direct presentation. Buckley regards the idea of the central relationship being 'sexless' as 'nonsense', though he significantly locates its sexuality not in overt expression, but 'at root, at depth' [p. 18]. As historians have had to deal with the doubleness of nineteenth-century society, with its moral and mannered surface and its concealed dimensions of vice and violence, so nineteenth-century texts lend themselves to being read for an analogous doubleness. When charted, those sexual undercurrents may often seem the more startling as a consequence of surface reticence.

Freud argued that what previous centuries called demonic possession, modern thought could interpret as neurosis; *Wuthering Heights* clearly contains a rich texture of the 'demonic' awaiting understanding as the human neurotic [see Kenney]. In this context, Lockwood's experience in the panelled bed has received particular attention. The reader quite understands from the narrative that Lockwood is a timorous lover; but it is left to Lockwood's possession by spirits, to his tantalisingly cryptic dreams to image his sexual repression most fully – and to psychoanalytical exegesis, such as Fine's, Kovel's or Wion's to articulate significances. A reading synthesised from such approaches might take the following form. In his first dream Lockwood is embarrassed by his lack of a 'staff' (as opposed to the dream-Joseph's 'boastfully flourishing a heavy-headed cudgel'); without such a staff, it seems, Lockwood will never 'get into the house', never 'gain admittance into my own residence'. The phallic character of these anxieties, envies, desires and understood rights of entry is complemented by the latent sexual identity of the 'house' or chapel he temporarily enters in his dream: 'it lies in a hollow, between two hills: an elevated hollow, near a swamp' (p. 21). From this house he is forcibly ejected, branded for his behaviour there by an oppressive religious and moral authority as the man who has committed the unpardonable sin (in this reading, attempting or contemplating sexual penetration). Such a conceit of the body as landscape, with play on the location of the genitals, has conscious precedents in English poetry, notably in Shakespeare's *Venus and Adonis* – a poem very much concerned not only with an inhibited male lover, but with the place, fulfilment and cost of sexuality in human love.

Like the first, Lockwood's second dream is also about attempted entry, and to that extent about sexual fear and guilt. A male neurosis about being trapped by the vulva in the sexual act is patterned in Lockwood's hand being so firmly grasped by the dream-Cathy after his fist has broken through the window. Guilt at the sexual act so imaged, the breaking of the hymen (the window) and the related loss of blood, is patterned in the rubbing to and fro of the child's wrist 'till the blood ran down and soaked the bed-clothes' (p. 23). The cry which echoes through the episode is 'let me in', a cry emanating from Lockwood's own frustration but projected onto the dream-Cathy; however, in dream as in life Lockwood's sense of inadequacy causes him to retreat from sexual encounter, to detumefy and 'shrink icily into himself' (p. 4) almost as soon as he has initiated relationship as a possibility, stopping his ears (like Odysseus against the Sirens' songs) while attempting to seal up (with a 'pyramid' (p. 23) – a tomb – of books) the principal orifice threatening his peace of mind. While the first dream figures the mechanics of repression in society and the inculcation of guilt, the second figures the autonomous workings of a regulatory guilt fully internalised. Meanwhile, Cathy's sexual being is firmly established for the reader through the role of the dream-Cathy.

Such interpretations of Lockwood's anxious dreams – contrasting with, say, Van Ghent's estimate of the 'gratuitous' violence of an 'emotionally unmotivated' character [p. 196] –

as of Linton's contemptible stance as husband, and Hindley's dangerous psychology as widower, suggest the novel positions the reader to recognise male sexuality as problematical, to be repelled by its stiffening and disguise through social, legal and institutional supports, and to be aware of the ease with which woman risks becoming, in such a context, victim of, rather than partner in, sexuality. Although some entirely valid fears of the greater risks borne by women are apparent, sexuality itself does not emerge as the root problem in human affairs so much as its frustration, inhibition, crippling – its deflection into compensations evolving through the consoling or sadistic exercise of power in a male-centred society. Being positioned to hold deficiencies such as Lockwood's and Linton's in contempt, one might posit the symmetry of a positive celebration, perhaps similarly displaced, of sexuality striving for uncrippled expression. If so, one must clearly look again to Cathy and Heathcliff.

Moser, moving through and beyond Van Ghent's description of Heathcliff as 'essentially, anthropomorphised primitive energy' and Richard Chase's account of him as 'sheer dazzling sexual and intellectual force', finds in Heathcliff a dramatisation of the *id* itself:

> The primary traits which Freud ascribed to the id apply perfectly to Heathcliff: the source of psychic energy; the seat of the instincts (particularly sex and death); the essence of dreams; the archaic foundation of personality – selfish, asocial, impulsive. [Moser, p. 4]

Moser, like Kovel, focuses on a series of scenes involving Heathcliff, Cathy, usually an ineffective male (such as Edgar or Hindley), and disputes involving entry through a door or window: 'Heathcliff always wins and the images suggest that the victory is a sexual conquest' [p. 5]. (Kovel, like Wion, emphasises such episodes as embodying a desire for return to the womb, to that 'maternal body' [p. 31] by which Heathcliff was originally abandoned.) Moser concludes that following the episode in which Edgar fails to throw Heathcliff out of the Grange, Cathy's 'sexual frustration' at Edgar's physical inadequacy, as shown up by Heathcliff (who eventually uses a poker to force a passage), 'clearly contributes' [p. 7] to her almost immediate collapse. Time and again, in such episodes,

Heathcliff is presented as controlling or attaining possession of keys, symbols of sexual capacity. On such grounds Moser describes the novel not at all as 'sexless' but as 'a passionate paean to *Eros*' [p. 12].

Not all critics delight in such readings. Allott included Moser's argument among those which 'promote a wasteful expenditure of time, ink and paper in refuting what no one in their senses would take seriously in the first place' [p. 29]; Lane ironically expressed surprise that no 'American professor' had yet found 'an anagram of sexual symbolism' [p. 188] in Catherine lazing in her cradle of tree-boughs – although Ward, back in 1900, could see Emily Brontë as an innocent writer 'who, in a world of sex and passion, has invented a situation charged with the full forces of both' [*cit.* Allott, 1970, p. 109]. Clearly, Heathcliff and Cathy have been in some danger of being diminished as images of humanity as much through their being read exclusively as animations of sexual principles as through their being accounted 'sexless'. But most problematical are such accounts' implications of Brontë the unconscious artist, the neurotic writer, a woman and a text explained by a psychology itself arguably dominated by male definitions of norms. Feminism's argument with Freud has understandably encouraged other frameworks to explain Emily's creative 'deviancy': Davies has recently turned to theories of perception and brain function to offer a positive account of Emily's 'sinistrality' of hand and 'dextrality' of mind as source of her rebellious and 'minority view of reality' [p. 12].

Cathy and Heathcliff's relationship may well be read as non-sexual or only limitedly sexual, yet the existence of a space for its climactic fulfilment in some terms can be agreed upon. However, as I shall develop the point in the 'Appraisal', the representation of sexual fulfilment which might have occupied such a space is displaced via a process whereby beds are transformed into coffins [D. Smith], where bodies become ghosts, where sexual maturity and the little death of orgasm are figured by other rites of passage, by dying and the convulsion of death itself, with death reworked not as annihilation or as Christian salvation, but as a new, continuous, and fulfilling existential state – not surprisingly leaving the characters' 'preliminary' relationship in life to appear as childlike or adolescent.

As with the coding of Lockwood's problems in dream, the supernatural gothic offers an alternative literary dimension to social realism within which a resolution to Cathy and Heathcliff's desires can be coded, examined and celebrated, a resolution which for one reason or another (cultural decorum/inexperience/personal reticence/repression/social paradox/artistic judgement) resisted direct formulation. Yet in this resolution the ambiguous connotations of death as loss as well as transcendence, the collision of a stark human reality with literary code, make such a displaced celebration of fulfilment – if that is what it is – intensely problematical. As Charlotte observed of 'Ellis Bell', 'he broaches ideas which strike my sense as much more daring than practical; his reason may be in advance of mine, but it certainly often travels a different road' [*cit.* Allott, 1970, p. 31].

A Novel is a Novel/is an Author/is a Reader

The teasing appeal of pattern in the verbal texture of *Wuthering Heights* made it a prime candidate for attention when formalist critics first started applying to novels techniques of analysis initially developed in connection with poetry. In America, two essays by Schorer partly devoted to *Wuthering Heights* [1948; 1949] achieved a seminal status in formalist criticism at large, while in England the inclusion of an essay on *Wuthering Heights* by Klingopulos in a famous series entitled 'The Novel as Dramatic Poem' posted notice of the responsiveness of Emily Brontë's novel to formalist strategy. These essays, and many that followed in their wake, stressed the 'poetic' qualities of *Wuthering Heights*, an observation now commonplace. However, that original emphasis on the 'poetic' should to some extent be recognised as a polemical gesture signalling the methodological breakthrough involved in transposing a particular critical technique from the field of poetry to the novel.

Formalist criticism focused attention on the demonstrable characteristics of words on the page, on the patterning of language in lexis, in metaphor, image-clusters and symbolism. Klingopulos's, Langman's, Buckley's or Cott's essays (the latter examining just the last sentence of the novel), directed a new attention to the perception of rhythm, irony [Jordan], and ambiguity in the language of fiction, greatly enhancing appreciation of the range and subtlety of Emily Brontë's prose, its restraint as well as its energy and elevation, and so augmented the range of interpretations of *Wuthering Heights*.

Schorer's fundamental contention was that a novel is a constructed image of life in a distinct medium, and that the first task of the critic is to understand the structure of that image as shaped in language. Form and content are one within such a perspective; the words the novelist uses must be appreciated against a background of other language-choices not made; style itself must be understood as the 'body of meaning' of the artefact. Discussion of the content of novels – events, plots, characters, themes – without reference to that verbal texture and tone which 'in themselves state and define themes and meanings' [1948, p. 68], is deemed inadequate and insensitive to the nature of the artwork.

Schorer argued that the language of *Wuthering Heights* testified to the novel's 'sphere of significant experience', and so teased out what he saw as the force of metaphor in the text, showing how 'the fierce life of animals and the relentless life of the elements – fire, wind, water' inform many of Emily Brontë's analogies. Human actions, responses and states of being, he found, were captured in the novel in a rhetoric suggesting 'the activities of the landscape', a language of wind, cloud and water, of floods, deluges, torrents and clouds, articulated in and by verbs of violent movement. (Readers who recall many more landscapes and storms than the novel actually contains *have* actually encountered them, but in the text's metaphors.) In short, he described 'a rhetorical texture where everything is at a pitch from which it can only subside', together with an 'antithetical chorus' of quietness and peace, finding expression in, for example, Nelly's frequent warnings to 'Hush!', the moths 'fluttering' over Heathcliff's grave on the last page, and in those creative rhythms of the seasons which through their cycles guarantee nature's permanence as against the individual's impermanence. For Schorer, Heathcliff's harsh 'singleness' of identity and action, lacking any alternation with the gentle, guarantees his destruction. The patterns of language shape the terms of the characters' fates and the novel's meaning within an autonomous artwork [1949, pp. 544–50]. Schorer's reading provided a more rigorous basis for talking about the centrality of nature as living force and ultimate value in the text, a force and value to which favoured characters are integrally attuned as they escape to the moors and brave its storms, while others retreat to firesides, laze on sofas or lock themselves away in libraries.

Schorer's [1949] strategy, still so much an element of critical method in its insistence on 'close reading' that it now risks appearing unremarkable, is in some ways a model of procedure, and certainly in the laying out of evidence. Its influence sprang from its elevation of language as medium and the promise arising of a self-contained discipline of literary analysis concerned with the autonomous text. Yet how does the selection of a matrix for study emerge? Although counting the recurrence of textual features has occasionally been espoused as a means to establishing the relative 'importance' of a text's features, without better criteria, or without the operation of some larger framework of thought explicitly pre-selecting specific elements of language use for study, such selection risks being less a free process of discovery than a rationalisation of presuppositions in which ideological assumptions are only concealed, not absent. Schorer's procedure was indeed followed by critics pursuing other metaphors and motifs who came to different conclusions about the novel's organising structures and meaning. The history of formalist approaches to *Wuthering Heights* can thus be seen as a history of the tracing through of different matrices, often illuminating and quite viable in themselves, yet competing for an elusive primacy, seeking assent as constituting *the* 'sphere of significant experience', *the* principle of unity and meaning. In practice such primacy can hardly be conceded to any one matrix, if only because others are so evidently capable of being elaborated with some degree of validity. Moreover, perceived patterns in the text resistant to commonsense interpretations could prove amenable to, say, psychoanalytical or mythopoeic explanation, eroding the claims of formalism to autonomy. The weight of significance Schorer found in natural imagery – or Cecil with his 'storm' and 'calm' – Van Ghent found in the use of windows, in the opposition of insides and outsides, in darkness and light, and from these features she elaborated her larger thesis concerning Cathy and Heathcliff's escape into a dark otherness of the soul with cosmic resonance. Gose found a central opposition in the 'heath' and the 'hearth'; MacKibben, a central pattern in images of books; Thompson a crucial pattern in images of pain offering psychoanalytical interest, in 'cutting, stabbing and choking', and 'throttling, suffocating or strangling' [p. 70] (although tunnel vision on the subject resulted in his recording Linton *literally* torturing cats whose claws and teeth have been pulled). The essential technique, for all its orthodoxy in the 1950s and 60s, was attacked by Doheny as an activity driven by professional academic pressures to publish, and for reducing *Wuthering Heights* in particular to 'a mine of phrases . . . to be worked, to be sorted, to be classified and forged into decorative bric-a-brac' [p. 21] – at the cost of understanding the novel's concern with the human predicament.

In practice critics found ways of living with the diverse conclusions of formalism. Reviewing debate about *Wuthering Heights* Watson [1949a] observed:

> Never, probably, will an interpretation of *Wuthering Heights* be made which will satisfy all people for all time, for a masterpiece of art has a life of its own which changes, develops, and unfolds as the generations pass. [p. 262]

The desire to see a single agreed account of the novel's meaning and value formulated is clearly there: the observation that '*probably*' no such interpretation will appear leaves just enough space for the pleasant possibility that it *might*. But, meanwhile, as the generations of readers 'pass', the stillness of *Wuthering Heights* as 'masterpiece' remains (like Keats' Grecian Urn), unfolding different layers of its inherent meaning to the generations like the layers of an onion. If debate cannot at any moment practically push through to the assumed unifying meaning constructed by the author, embodied in the text and potentially available to all readers, then the problem, it seems, lies less with critical methodology or assumptions about unity of meaning than in the happy capacity of the masterpiece constantly to surprise the student with its inherent depth of organisation.

This stance may be contrasted with a characteristic poststructuralist viewpoint [Matthews] from the mid 1980s:

> Perhaps the millions of interpretive words which have come to encase

this love story measure the incapacity of Catherine and Heathcliff to speak for themselves. [p. 29]

This voice no longer speaks out of a world of critical debate concerned with the revelation of some meaning secreted in the text by the author, awaiting extraction or elegant expression by critics working cumulatively and homogeneously down the ages. In this world reading and debate may well no longer be concerned with identifying or quantifying 'masterpieces' at all; value has shifted away from the idea of an inputting author ('genius'), as from an achieved artwork ('masterpiece') and from a prescribed idea of a unitary culture within which the text must live ('tradition'); the model of literary operation has become one of readers reading texts, reinventing the text's meaning as they read. The nature and quality of readings depend on the readers, and in the permutations of class, gender, race and nationality there is a potentially infinite number with their own validity. Pluralism has moved from being a liberal concession to being an axiom of expectation. Catherine and Heathcliff are 'incapable' of speaking for themselves, of being read out of the text; it is the reader whose act of reading must articulate them and rescue the text from its own muteness. There is little point in talking about the author of the text as Emily Brontë, for the reader has become the author, inserting her/himself into the points of tension in the text, seeking not the satisfaction of the unified interpretation of the work understood as a communication between author and all readers, but rather his/her own record of textual pleasures, contradictions and discontinuities, experiences of inclusion and exclusion, and collisions with both the text that is there and its perceived omissions and evasions [Barthes]. Interpretation thus 'encases' the text with the activity of a reader who is unique but for those cultural conditions which qualify her/his uniqueness. Debate is still possible to the extent that readings still require justification (and can still be wrong, inaccurate, inconsistent), and such grounds as one reader shares with another define constituencies with their own possibilities of convergent readings; moreover, the attempt to understand the other reader, or to be understood by the other reader, still has an imperative attaching to it.

If honesty to reading experiences, together with doubts

about the politico-cultural implications of what F. R. Leavis dubbed the 'common pursuit' of a text's meaning and value has left criticism and critics fragmented, this occurs in a situation where unity, within the text and within criticism, is no longer necessarily seen as a good. In the important discussions of *Wuthering Heights* by Kermode and by Miller [1982], it is the novel's very resistance to any one interpretation attempting to close down discussion, its capacity and durability as a text to allow the generation of a plurality of readings, which warrants its description as a 'classic'. 'The secret truth about *Wuthering Heights*', observes Miller, 'is that there is no [one] secret truth', no 'univocal principle of explanation' [p. 51].

If criticism is what cultures do to texts, what a culture does to texts is as much a consequence of the culture being the way it is as of the text being the way it is [see Eagleton, 1983]. Historians of critical debate may well be surprised how often advances in debate are translations of perceptions from one critical metalanguage into another, where what is as much at stake as any wholly fresh insight into the particular text is the viability or resilience of the critical metalanguage concerned and its underlying ideology, the capacity of its forms and concepts and methods to achieve elegant formulations in the context of another experimental operation, and thus to augment themselves.

A window stands open at the Heights – just a window in a Yorkshire house. But it stands open to allow Lockwood and Nelly to look in and narrate. The wind which binds the house and its inhabitants to Nature blows through it. It has provided escape for the flight of the soul after death – to Hell, to a new Heaven – and a focus for the attention of ghosts. The landscape it frames has provided a space in which characters can construct themselves through desire. It has been a passageway to the dark otherness of the cosmos. It has been a site where sexual inadequacy, sexual potency, and desires for return to childhood, and to the womb, have defined themselves. It has been an entry, an exit, a division, a reconciliation. For Matthews it is a reflexive symptom of the text's concern with frames and framing as a condition of textuality and reading, an enactment, like the framing narrative techniques, of those boundaries which define the spaces within which writing can occur [p. 57]. If critics have become aware of literature less as a realm of universal values than of ideology, the corollary is that debate itself, in and through history, has also constituted ideology. While the further illumination of the text in such a politics has been an end, so too has been the establishment of method by which it may be achieved. The window is still open – and, among other things, a sore temptation to burglars (though at least one window there has its hook soldered into its staple . . .).

PART TWO
APPRAISAL
'Wuthering Heights': Passion and Property

Houses and Titles

Wuthering Heights has a familiar form of title. In many novels' title-formula an individual's name figures in a way which has become a resonant convention: Moll Flanders, Tom Jones, David Copperfield, Mrs Dalloway. Such titles enact the novel's involvement as literary form with ideas about the integration of personality, and with assumptions about the centrality to human life, interaction and understanding, of the discrete subjective consciousness epitomised by the hero-figure of the Western liberal middle-class novel. In the case of *Wuthering Heights*, a tendency runs through Gothic and Romantic fiction into the High Victorian novel and beyond, for novels to be named after places, after buildings, after homes, after properties: Walpole's *The Castle of Otranto*, Peacock's *Crotchet Castle*, Jane Austen's *Northanger Abbey* and *Mansfield Park*, Dickens's *Bleak House*, Trollope's *Framley Parsonage*, Waugh's *Brideshead Revisited*. Perceiving the broad tendency, however, only highlights the subtly different connotations shadowing such terms as 'places, buildings, homes, properties', the tensions which lie immanent between the terms, and immanent in the novels.

Houses in novels constitute more than just the local habitations characters require within a realistic illusion. They may stand expressionistically for some intensity of experience, perhaps spatially localised and articulated through the discrete symbolic spaces of an Interpreter's House (the madwoman in the attic, the secret garden, something nasty in the woodshed), or function as properties in dispute, potential prizes and justifications, raising and ultimately used in closure to clarify spiritual, moral and material rights to possession. (In Henry James's title '*The Spoils of Poynton*', home is booty.) Indeed, named properties contain within themselves an absence begging completion with the name of that owner whose rights of ownership define the house *as* property, rather than just as place, building or home.

Intensity of experience and the rights to possession are the themes signalled by the very title-formula of *Wuthering Heights*. Northanger Abbey allows Catherine Morland's Gothic imaginings free rein, imaginings already nourished by precisely such reading as *The Castle of Otranto* and *The Castle of Wolfenbach*. But at Mansfield Park it is pointedly the moral ownership of the great country house which is ripe for appropriation or rejuvenation by competing social forces. In *Bleak House*, the house of society teeters between the alternative conditions of Tom-All-Alone's decay and the sunny cottage, the un-bleak house, ultimately inhabited by the heroine and her husband. Who, the novels explore, should rightly inhabit a Framley Parsonage, a Barchester Towers, a Howards End, a Brideshead, properties which may carry symbolic overtones of the nation itself, of a favoured ideal of civilisation, of some mode of fulfilled living? While such houses may lack the programmatic allegory of Spenser's Houses of Pride and Holiness, they may still be houses of the mind, of the emotions, of desire, while simultaneously brick-and-mortar houses of people in society, built, bought, sold and inherited. With the Gothic examples of novels named after properties the emphasis expectedly falls upon houses as foci of intense experience, while, broadly speaking, the balance shifts towards the guidance, control and possession of property as one moves into the Victorian examples and beyond.

Indeterminacy in Emily Brontë's title leaves her novel poised on a fracture-line between these generic associations. No particular kind of dwelling, no particular social status of house, is immediately specified. It is not a castle, or a hall, or an abbey, or a park, or a parsonage or towers, or a 'grange' like Thrushcross, or even explicitly a house, or indeed even the farm as which it does actually function. It is 'Wuthering Heights', a name evading both social and visual connotations as far as any designated house is concerned. Indeed, the name can function purely topographically within an ascending scale of landscape running through, say, Gimmerton Marsh, Wuthering Heights and Penistone Crags. The word 'wuthering', unfamiliar to most readers outside this novel (as it also is to the *Oxford English Dictionary*), compounds uncertainty. For Lockwood, 'wuthering' is 'a significant provincial adjective descriptive of the atmospheric tumult to which its station is exposed in stormy weather' (p. 2); yet he may well be understood as merely mocking what he regards as a deviant local pronunciation of 'weathering'. Moreover, while 'Heights' suggests a ridge or promontory of a range of hills, the abstract dimension of the word's meaning does not disappear and so also conveys the ideas of heights of undefined intensity, heights of emotional tumult, heights – as it were – of 'wuthering'. In reading, the word is impressively evocative yet ultimately elusive in meaning, a Moby Dick among words. The house may materialise out of the title in all its solidity as property and object of contest, as a way of living and a means of life. But then interior spaces materialise, 'house' and back-kitchen, garret and cellar, hearth and windows, doors and passages, skylight and closet-bed – locations in an exploded diagram of human feeling. Davies has recently written of this 'interiority', with its 'compression of psychic energy', as resembling the 'intramural structuring of the mind itself' [p. 3].

Within the title are the major contesting themes in the history of the novel's discussion – passion and property – and the themes most needing correlation in reading *Wuthering Heights*.

The Nameless Man

Heathcliff enters the *story* of *Wuthering Heights* as a ragged child rescued from a 'houseless' existence (p. 35). Yet, in the very first sentence, he enters the *text* as 'landlord' (p. 1). Three chapters pass before Nelly's narrative disturbs what the reader initially gleans of Heathcliff's social identity with memories of his first arrival at the Heights. This return to the beginning of the story opens a chasm of information and interpretation stretching between the polarities of Heathcliff as adult 'landlord' and 'houseless' child – as someone lacking even the anomalous social position later conferred on him with the name 'Heathcliff'. Bridging that chasm, that tantalising disruption of commonsense social and economic expectations, becomes a dynamic of *Wuthering Heights*. For the contemporary reader in particular, in the era of European revolution, this translation of Heathcliff needed explanation, embodying as it did disturbing possibilities of breakdown in a social order familiarly guaranteed by watertight processes in the transmission of property within class and family.

As street-urchin Heathcliff barely enjoys being called 'someone'. Characters' recognition of his humanity is qualified by his categorisation as 'gipsy', as essentially outside and at war with a society of mutually reinforcing moral and economic relationships. The insult 'gipsy' carried a stigma in the eighteenth and early nineteenth centuries which was in proportion to that society's anchorage in the stabilities of landownership. Heathcliff's appearance in a rural economy, mouthing 'gibberish, that nobody could understand . . . as good as dumb' (p. 35), perceived as some rootless, perhaps racially distinct, linguistically separate, proletarian offspring of industrial Liverpool, is a manifold eruption of the outside into the centre.

Emily Brontë was writing *Wuthering Heights* during the Irish famine of 1845–6 when, Gérin [1966] reports, 'the newspapers of the day were filled with reports of the Irish immigrants crowding the docks of Liverpool in search of food and dying in their hundreds in the cellars of the foul Liverpool tenements before help came, leaving an orphan population scouring the gutters'. The same commentator sees the lack of *explicit* connection between Heathcliff and such events as indicating Emily Brontë's determination 'to surround every phase of his life with mystery, to spread a supernatural aura about him from the first' [p. 14]. But how curious, then, to specify Liverpool – Ireland's gateway to England, situated just a long walk away from Wuthering Heights – for the Irish famine, appearing to Victorian eyes as one of the greatest calamities in world history, was part of what Liverpool necessarily connoted in the Hungry Forties. In 1845 the Devon Commission began investigating the byzantine relationships between Irish landlords and tenants, a major factor in the peasantry's vulnerability to poverty and famine. In no other European country did so few landlords own so much land, nor were the tenants so oppressed, as a consequence of serial subtenancy. Such was landlord–tenant conflict, aggravated by famine, that in the late 1840s the Home Secretary acted to repress crimes (principally murder) against 'every class and description of landowner' in Ireland. The Commission also warned of 'Irish ignorance, beggary, and disease, with all their contagion, physical and moral . . . intermingling with the British population' and of the difficulty of preventing 'the half-starved Irish peasantry from crossing the Channel, and seeking employment even at low-wages, and forming a pestiferous Irish quarter in every town and city'. Emily Brontë could easily have avoided any such associations by having Heathcliff found abandoned on those moors which have so fuelled 'mysterious' and 'supernatural' interpretations of the novel. As it is, as Kettle insisted, the Liverpool connection cannot be shaken off, nor can those refugees with whom the whole Brontë family, with their own Irish roots, would have inevitably felt connected, though doubtless problematically. One cannot insist that Heathcliff *is* Irish, or that landlord-tenant conflict is necessarily responsible for his condition; besides, historically he is a child of the 1760s rather than the 1840s: but for Brontë writing and her earliest readers brooding on the making – and the threat – of Heathcliff, such associations were all too available.

Heathcliff's non-belonging is also conveyed through epithets associating him with devils and demons. Although this imagery has been read as signalling that Heathcliff actually *is* a demon (see the fourth section of the 'Survey'), or as reflecting the characters' instinctive and proper recognition of his moral evil, it can also be less sensationally understood as the characters resorting to some ready and authoritative categorisation of the alien, thus capturing not so much Heathcliff's absolute devilishness as their own socially relative hostility towards the alien, and their confirmation of his status by word-magic. (To be outside society's commonsense values is to be perceived as a devil, a demon, a gipsy, insane: this is the process of populist self-definition, which – as in the rhetoric of today's tabloid press – draws the boundaries of a society and its values, and confirms its own rightness by converting the otherness of the excluded into the most unacceptable, unredeemable otherness envisaged in its language.)

As a pronoun Heathcliff is initially merely 'it' – a piece of abandoned property which should have 'belonged' to an 'owner' (p. 35); he has spiralled down through levels of depersonalisation to a point of negation lower than even the indignity of constituting a possession. To some degree he achieves human and social definition, is translated from 'it' into 'he', through being 'christened' (p. 36) 'Heathcliff' by the Earnshaws. But this occurs during a narrative hiatus when the witness Nelly is temporarily absent. No actual ceremony of social or religious validity is reported and the reader is left to assume that there has been none. Similarly, any question of formal or legal adoption is left in abeyance.

Naming is a sensitive issue, for names are counters for legal and personal identity. In referring to her death, Heathcliff is unable in his agony to pronounce Cathy's Christian name, and resorts to the palliative of talking about 'she' (p. 166). Cathy and Edgar's child (who answers to both 'Cathy' and 'Catherine', but cannot abide Linton's use of the servile formula 'Miss Catherine') presents more complications:

> It was named Catherine, but he never called it the name in full, as he had never called the first Catherine short, probably because Heathcliff had a habit of doing so. The little one was always Cathy: it formed to him a distinction from the mother, and yet, a connection with her. (p. 191)

Thereby hangs a dilemma. In only attempting consistency, critics risk favouring either Heathcliff or Edgar by referring to the woman each loves as respectively either 'Cathy' or 'Catherine'. (Her naming is the first of her divisions.) (In this study – without escaping the dilemma – I normally refer to the mother as 'Cathy' and the daughter as 'Catherine'.)

The name Heathcliff acquires has precedent as the Christian name 'of a son who died in childhood' (p. 36), though whether older or younger than Hindley is unclear. In practice Heathcliff's name oscillates between being a sign of community with God and a sign of community in family. It 'serves' him, observes Nelly Dean, 'both as Christian and surname' (p. 36), but rather than a dual function there is an oscillation resulting in the name never satisfactorily serving him either way. It only 'serves' in the sense of 'making do': he is certainly never wholly integrated in name as, say, 'Heathcliff Earnshaw'. This is significant, for in *Wuthering Heights* names do double as Christian and surnames (for example, 'Isabella *Linton*' and '*Linton* Heathcliff'), and recur as if generated within a restricted morphology. (Heathcliff's childhood companion 'Catherine Earnshaw' becomes 'Catherine Linton' when she marries Edgar, while her daughter 'Catherine Linton' in turn becomes 'Catherine Heathcliff' when she marries Isabella's son by Heathcliff, and beyond the last page of the novel is set to become the new 'Catherine Earnshaw' in marrying Hareton. Even the 'Hareton Earnshaw' of 1800 is prefigured by the builder of the Heights, the 'Hareton Earnshaw' of 1500 [*cf.* Kermode; Kavanagh].) Yet in all this dance of names (foregrounded by Lockwood's confusions during his first visits to the Heights) the particular combination 'Heathcliff Earnshaw' remains the identity of the dead son alone, and Heathcliff's onomastic inheritance lies crucially crippled, more a memorial to the incorporated dead than any liberating legacy to the excluded living. Later, when Heathcliff is brought up smartly against his deficiencies of birth, name and expectation, Nelly proffers the consolations of fantasy:

> Tell me whether you don't think yourself rather handsome? I'll tell you, I do. You're fit for a prince in disguise. Who knows, but your father was Emperor of China, and your mother an Indian queen, each of them able to buy up, with one week's income, Wuthering Heights and Thrushcross Grange together? And you were kidnapped by wicked sailors and brought to England. Were I in your place, I would frame high notions of my birth. (p. 56)

The reader is teased to expect some revelation of Heathcliff's aristocratic parentage (as in many a foundling-narrative), but Nelly's blithe remarks also expose Heathcliff to some potent ideas. That his parents may have been Emperor of China and an Indian queen is far-fetched stuff; that he may have been kidnapped is less far-fetched, though still the stuff of romance; that he might acquire Wuthering Heights and Thrushcross

Grange is just as fantastic a scenario to Nelly, but one actually dependent on no dream of the past or the future for realisation. A prince in disguise is one likelihood; the possibility of 'buying up' two properties – of thereby inserting oneself into a self-enclosed system of birth, marriage and inheritance – is, while remote, quite another. Heathcliff, who later mocks Isabella for picturing him as 'a hero of romance' (p. 150), takes only the most practical consolation from Nelly's words.

As a child, Cathy can half-consciously review a range of present and speculative identities through which to construct herself; Lockwood finds her scratchings on a window-ledge at Wuthering Heights: 'The writing . . . was nothing but a name repeated in all kinds of characters, large and small – *Catherine Earnshaw*, here and there varied to *Catherine Heathcliff*, and then again to *Catherine Linton*'. If, as 'the air swarmed with Catherines' (p. 17), this musing indicates the specific terms of Cathy's dilemma, located within a discourse about identity, gender, marriage and class ([present self/future spinster]/wife 1/wife 2), Heathcliff's dilemma, primarily within a discourse about identity and social incorporation, revolves around a shortage of names. 'Mr Heathcliff' is an awkward compromise with conventional surnames. The title 'Mr' highlights the surrogacy of 'Heathcliff' as surname. The initial oddness of Isabella Linton becoming 'Isabella Heathcliff' through marriage is symptomatic of the strains created between Heathcliff's singular naming and the horizontal institution of marriage – just as strains are also automatically created with the vertical structures of property inheritance. (Isabella later refers to the 'ridiculous, contemptible, degrading title of Mrs Heathcliff' (p. 181).) Moreover, to the extent that 'Heathcliff' is a Christian name, the formula 'Mr Heathcliff' (especially when used by servants) resembles the formula for a son awaiting his patrimony – e.g. 'Mr John', or 'Mr Frederick' – ironically suggesting that Heathcliff is in legal terms doomed to eternal non-inheritance. Not knowing Joseph's, Zillah's, Michael's, Mary's, Robert's or Jenny's surnames merely confirms their unchanging status as servants, their marginal relationship to the socially stabilising structures of family and inheritance. To know only Lockwood's surname is quite enough, for it locates him among the property-owning classes whose surnames confirm their part in structures limiting and enabling the transfer of property. (Lockwood *rents* Thrushcross Grange for leisure purposes, flitting from London to the seacoast or the moors as he fancies. His mother may have doubted his ever having 'a comfortable home' (p. 4) – that is, a fulfilled relationship with a wife – but there is no danger of his not having a house.) 'Kenneth' may also be confidently understood as the local doctor's surname, despite the ambiguity. Membership of a professional and owning class guarantees that 'Mr Kenneth' – 'plain, rough man' though he be (p. 130) – is not a problematic name like 'Mr Heathcliff'. Ellen Dean, with her formal 'Mrs Dean' and her diminutive 'Nelly', is equipped for a range of social situations (making credible her mobility as witness and narrator – and confirming the complexity of her class-position as character). Heathcliff, however, can often not know on what basis of friendship, relationship, patronage, formality, respect or acceptance he is being treated when simply addressed as 'Heathcliff'; it is the name used by his lover, the name by which he is commanded and cursed – and the name under which he attempts to insert himself into an owning society. His name is an indeterminate space within which he moves in search of definition, but also a constant reminder of the unsatisfactory fit between himself and the codes of a society denying him incorporation. When Heathcliff calls Edgar Linton, who has no such problems, 'the cipher at the Grange', it is a heartfelt insult. As the first page of the novel confirms, the exchange of names and status between gentlemen is the first formality of polite relationship. Yet Heathcliff does not volunteer his: he merely nods in acceptance of Lockwood's use of it. Heathcliff's name is also a reminder of the paradoxes of desire: to aspire to the social identity of a 'Heathcliff Earnshaw' would bring with it some more explicit form of brother-sister relationship with Cathy, giving more substance to that taboo of incest often sensed hovering in or behind the text.

With Heathcliff's death, Nelly no longer feels the need to make concessions to half-truths and compromises prudent during his lifetime: it is now quite clear to her, in dream and in reality, that Heathcliff has simply lacked a surname:

> I tracked his existence over again, with grim variations; at last, picturing his death and funeral; of which, all I can remember is being exceedingly

> vexed at having the task of dictating an inscription for his monument and consulting the sexton about it; and, as he had no surname, and we could not tell his age, we were obliged to content ourselves with the single word 'Heathcliff'. That came true, we were. If you enter the kirkyard, you'll read on his headstone only that, and the date of his death. (p. 330)

This for the character whose whole world becomes Cathy's inscription, 'a dreadful collection of *memoranda* that she did exist, and that I have lost her!' (p. 324; my italics). Hareton may suffer temporary dispossession, but 'his' name is literally carved – Christian and surname – in the fabric of Wuthering Heights, a title to possession waiting to underwrite his inheritance. Hareton cannot read that name over his own doorway until the stimulus of pleasing Catherine spurs him on towards literacy. In mocking his illiteracy, Catherine and Linton do not decipher the inscription for him, though Catherine senses its importance ('It's some damnable writing', he answered. 'I cannot read it'. 'Can't read it?' cried Catherine, 'I can read it . . . it's English . . . but I want to know why it is there' (p. 220).) Joseph can instil into Hareton 'a pride of name, and of his lineage' (p. 196), but it is only after Hareton can read the inscription, can recognise his name and why it is there, that he shows a rebellious force. Indeed he demands his own space ('Get to thy own room! . . . thou shalln't keep me out of this'), and throws Linton and Catherine into the kitchen. Joseph delights in Hareton's now knowing 'as weel as Aw do, who sud be t'maister yonder' (p. 251).

Other inscriptions crystallise disruptions of inheritance. Linton and Catherine, wanting to play ball, discover two old ones in a cupboard, marked 'C' and 'H'. Catherine innocently reports:

> I wished to have the C., because that stood for Catherine, and the H. might be for Heathcliff, his name; but the bran came out of H., and Linton didn't like it. (p. 248)

The 'C' does stand for Catherine; the ball belonged to Cathy, and there is indeed an aptness in Catherine now possessing it. The 'H', however, most probably stood for 'Hindley', and in her misreading Catherine unwittingly re-enacts her dead uncle's dispossession by Heathcliff, just as she unconsciously aids Heathcliff's further plans by pursuing Linton. There is a dry irony in the disintegration of the ball which Linton falsely 'inherits' on the strength of its misread inscription.

The problems of inscribing Heathcliff in stone which Nelly dreams, echo those Heathcliff faces from a society unprepared to inscribe his existence within its fabric, a society able to accommodate writing his death, but which neither records for him any clear facts of birth or name which might legitimise his place within its text, nor grants him any effective substitute for them. As Nelly tells Lockwood with some pointedness in beginning her story, she knows all about Heathcliff, 'except where he was born, and who were his parents, and how he got his money, at first' (p. 33).

A Cuckoo's History: the Landlord as Hero

The story Nelly tells is just one of those capable of being constructed out of the book's events. 'The' story, as Nelly narrates it, is formed by her understanding of what 'the' story actually is.

That Nelly is a partial narrator whose values colour her narrative is now widely agreed (see the third section of the 'Survey'). Other characters – Lockwood, Zillah, Isabella, Heathcliff, Catherine – occasionally narrate, but thereby only emphasise the scale of Nelly's role. Lockwood suggests many distinct frameworks for Nelly's narrative, any of which – given appropriate editing and extension – might show order and significance (of different kinds) within essentially the same events. He suggests autobiography ('"You have lived here a considerable time", I commenced; "did you not say sixteen years?"'); Nelly's life-story might filter the events of *Wuthering Heights* very differently in seeking their relevance to her own career and destiny. Lockwood angles for a framework based on Catherine – 'That pretty girl-widow, I should like to know her history' (p. 31) – a story which again promises differences to the one we have. With confusion about the relationships of Earnshaws, Lintons and Heathcliffs, a family saga is understandably proposed – 'Are they an old family?' (p. 32); but then Lockwood returns to Heathcliff ('He must have had some ups and downs in life to make him such a churl. Do you know anything of his history?'). Throughout Lockwood's probings Nelly responds to Heathcliff's name with most animation, and this question enables her to begin, 'waiting no further invitation to her story'. Lockwood invites the story not necessarily in any 'correct' form – but in one which Nelly accepts as meaningful: 'I know all about it', she replies, going on to define Heathcliff's story as 'a cuckoo's history' – a story of how the 'houseless' became the 'landlord', and one to be told out of a sympathy with those 'dunnocks' evicted from their nest by the invading 'cuckoo' (p. 33).

A nest is a bird's 'house', a protection against the elements; it is occupied by a pair; it is where young are reared, a centre of warm intimacy and domesticity, an image of life and harmony – as when Catherine 'nestles' in her favourite tree with its other 'tenants':

> From dinner to tea she would lie in her breeze-rocked cradle, doing nothing except singing old songs – my nursery lore – to herself, or watching the birds, joint tenants, feed and entice their young ones to fly, or nestling with closed lids, half thinking, half dreaming, happier than words can express. (p. 230)

A territory and a possession, a nest is defended and subject to depredation and even appropriation – at least by the cuckoo. The metaphor accretes meaning and poignancy from events and conversations as well as from Nelly's commentary. Catherine discovers that *her* nest, her childish but nevertheless personal property-space – a drawer of love-letters – has been raided:

> Never did any bird flying back to a plundered nest which it had left brim-ful of chirping young ones, express more complete despair in its anguished cries and flutterings, than she by her single 'Oh!' and the change that transfigured her late happy countenance. (p. 226)

Usually, Heathcliff is in the figure. Cathy says 'he'd crush you like a sparrow's egg, Isabella, if he found you a troublesome charge' (p. 102); Nelly agrees, characterising Heathcliff as 'a bird of bad omen: no mate for you' (p. 103). In a variation during her delirium – possibly a literal memory, but also a suggestive symbolic rendering of Heathcliff's assault on the 'ancient stock of the Earnshaws' and of his intervention between parent and child – Cathy recalls a lapwing's nest 'full of little skeletons. Heathcliff set a trap over it, and the old ones dare not come' (pp. 122–3). In another variation the nest as an image of domestic warmth, but simultaneously understood as a material possession (that is, 'belonging' to the *bird*), is used to establish how deeply Heathcliff has moved into the values of ownership. Catherine goes in search of moor-game simply 'to see whether they have made their nests yet' (p. 213). Suddenly reconfigured within a perspective of property rights (within which Hareton can be described as 'robbing our woods of pheasants'), Catherine's actions mutate in significance: 'moor-game' become 'grouse'; wild birds and their nests become part of the economy of landowners who rent out to such Lockwoods as desire to 'devastate the moors' (p. 305):

> Cathy had been caught in the fact of plundering, or, at least, hunting out the nests of the grouse.
> The Heights were Heathcliff's land, and he was reproving the poacher. (p. 213)

Just once, nest imagery conveys Heathcliff's anguish and defines *his* loss: as he awaits news of Cathy's death, Nelly sees 'a pair of ousels passing and repassing scarcely three feet from him, busy in building their nest, and regarding his proximity no more than that of a piece of timber' (p. 166).

Nelly's 'cuckoo's history' does not ignore the palimpsest stories invited by Lockwood, but essentially she tells a tale of property ownership, centred on Heathcliff. The context of the story-telling works to determine this. Nelly the *housekeeper* is narrating to Lockwood the new *tenant*; the housekeeper only knows Lockwood as tenant, while the tenant initially knows nothing about his 'human fixture and her satellites' (p. 30) beyond their role as housekeeper and servants. They only meet through these foregrounded social and economic roles, aspects of the pervasive operation of property as shaping factor in human interaction. The story of their landlord's houses, and how he has acquired the properties which the three of them occupy, bears upon the continuing property relationships of subject, teller and listener. It is, perhaps, the only story which Nelly and Lockwood can share with mutual engagement. Moreover, as they begin, the events from which the whole story and text of *Wuthering Heights* are drawn are incomplete. Heathcliff's finances are in the ascendant: he has 'nobody knows what money, and every year it increases' (p. 32); Hareton and Catherine's love story lies in the future; Heathcliff's will to manipulate shows no sign of weakening; his death is equally beyond prophecy. Heathcliff's present situation, against which the pattern of the past must be construed by any time-bound interpreter, is that of successful landlord, and just so does Nelly construct him and find his story worth telling. Again, despite his night at the Heights, Lockwood says nothing about ghosts and dreams; instead, he cues Nelly with a question about Heathcliff's wealth and why he 'let Thrushcross Grange and preferred living in a situation and residence so much inferior' (p. 32). This is tenant interrogating housekeeper rather than, say, the inquiry of a connoisseur of passion or of the supernatural.

Now the Heathcliff Nelly initially describes – 'close-handed', 'greedy', remaining at Wuthering Heights because he cannot bear to lose the 'few hundreds' (p. 32) accruing from Lockwood renting Thrushcross Grange – bears scant relation to the young Heathcliff she later introduces. Yet Lockwood's early visits corroborate Nelly's portrait. On his very first visit Lockwood encounters a chained gate manned by Heathcliff; on his second, the 'jealous' (p. 298) gate is still chained and the door is locked. Inside are other security measures. Heathcliff observes of one of the dogs that she is 'not kept for a pet' (p. 5), and keeping watch is a significant element of these working dogs' duties. Finding they have set upon Lockwood, Heathcliff explains 'They won't meddle with persons who touch nothing. . . . The dogs do right to be vigilant' (pp. 5–6). A startling image of the defensive tenor of life at the Heights, of its atmosphere of barely suppressed force in the service of property, occurs in Lockwood's description of Catherine Heathcliff resisting help in taking down a container: he records her turning on him with a male aggression and possessiveness, 'as a miser might turn, if anyone attempted to assist him in counting his gold' (p. 9). The economy of the Heights could well appear a miser's as far as outsiders are concerned, although the inhabitants enjoy a 'warm, cheerful apartment' and 'a plentiful meal' (p. 8). But Heathcliff keeps no 'accommodations for visitors' (pp. 14–15); there are no farm-boys to guide Lockwood through the snow. Jealous suspicion of the visitor rules. Lockwood is offered the unenviable prospect of sharing a bed with Hareton or Joseph, partly to dissuade him from staying, but also to ensure his surveillance during the night. On his third visit he immediately recognises that in the absence of Heathcliff, Hareton accompanies him indoors 'in the office of a watchdog, not as a substitute for the host' (p. 298). When Lockwood proposes sleeping in the main room, Heathcliff is frank: 'No, no! A stranger is a stranger, be he rich or poor – it will not suit me to permit anyone the range of the place while I am off guard!' Ironically, Lockwood rushes out angrily at his imputation, only to be accused by Joseph of 'staling t'lantern', and for the dogs ('Gnasher' and 'Wolf') to tackle him again (p. 15). Lockwood offers only a parodic threat to Heathcliff's silver tankards, but the overstated response Heathcliff exposes is illuminating. Next morning the siege mentality of the Heights further restricts Lockwood's movements: 'Keep out of the yard, though, the dogs are unchained; and the house – Juno mounts sentinel there – and – nay, you can only ramble about the steps and passages' (p. 26). This is the household regime of a landlord preoccupied with the increase and defence of what he has. If, as Jack suggests, Emily Brontë partially visualised the Heights in terms of Scott's castle-cum-house in *Waverley* with its turrets, loopholes and battlements – defences against 'any roving band of gipsies' (p. viii) – such themes of defence are also incarnate in Heathcliff's behaviour.

Lockwood's discomfort blooms in the gap between his expectations concerning the forms and rituals in which ownership is customarily dressed (and hidden) by his own class, and the stark facts of possession and defence, of inclusion and exclusion, as unceremoniously displayed by Heathcliff. Astonishingly, for Lockwood, his gentlemanly status does not activate any mechanism of class solidarity in Heathcliff and allay his suspicion. Instead, he has to experience security measures from an unaccustomed side of the fence.

His visits to the Heights Lockwood casts in the style of a polite visitor touring a country house. Constructing himself as the genteel traveller, the dilettante antiquarian, he accordingly constructs Heathcliff as the gentleman-landlord receiving the visit. However, he has to resort to ironising the house and the behaviour of its inhabitants, 'that pleasant family circle' (p. 12), when his social gambits are refused and his expectations frustrated. He tries to reflect with decorum on the name of the house, its situation and appearance. For valetudinarian friends he notes the 'bracing ventilation' and even compliments the 'architect' – a term more relevant to assessing a great country house than to understanding the practical priorities of Wuthering Heights as a building. Nevertheless, before entering, the visitor carefully notes prominent carvings and inscriptions, as if for his commonplace book: 'I would have made a few comments, and requested a short history of the place from the surly owner; but his attitude at the door appeared to demand my speedy entrance or complete departure' (pp. 2–3). Lockwood detects rudeness; but there are other motives in Heathcliff's predilection for locked doors.

Lockwood merely attempts to play out the conventions of property-visiting among his class, but flounders without Heathcliff's reciprocation. His blunders about people's relationships follow from Heathcliff omitting formal introductions (which would also have clarified individuals' social status). So with nowhere to go except deeper into the misdirection of his own ideology, Lockwood can only struggle on. The *penetralia* (inner chambers) which he anticipates resolve into a disturbingly singular and grammatically ironised '*penetralium*' – the one main room, or 'house' (p. 3). Isabella will also seek the parlour in vain: '"*Parlour!*" [Joseph] echoed sneeringly, "*parlour!* Nay, we've noa *parlours*. If yah dunnut loike wer company, they's maister's; un' if yah dunnut loike maister, they's us"' (p. 142). The expected lady's kittens resolve into a heap of dead rabbits.

Lockwood's persistence testifies to the paradoxical that he genuinely finds in Heathcliff, 'a dark-skinned gypsy in aspect, in dress and manners a gentleman' (p. 3). For Heathcliff *can* play the gentleman convincingly; eventually he even does enough by way of recognising Lockwood as guest and playing the polite conversational games his tenant desires for Lockwood to resolve on another visit. Lockwood does not necessarily misinterpret the 'prudential' motives for Heathcliff's sudden condescension (though he mistakes it as betokening the real Heathcliff). Lockwood knows polite behaviour and language when he encounters them – and especially in a reassuring exchange on the quasi-Horatian theme of rural retirement, part of a familiar drawing-room stock-in-trade (p. 6). Heathcliff does send Lockwood a brace of grouse during his illness, and is, moreover, 'charitable enough to sit at my bedside a good hour, and talk on some other subject than pills and draughts, blisters and leeches' (p. 90). Nelly assesses the adult Heathcliff as looking intelligent, having a dignified manner, and being 'quite divested of roughness' (p. 95). He has always had reserve.

Heathcliff *is* certainly the landlord, and, when tactically advisable, he can also *act* the gentleman. Usually, however, he is the landlord who in his siege mentality feels no compulsion to disguise the bald terms on which property ownership is sustained. Creditably or not, Isabella quickly adapts to surviving at Heathcliff's Wuthering Heights: she abandons her 'self-respect' (p. 140), declares that 'I'm not going to act the lady among you, for fear I should starve' (p. 141), and within hours of her arrival, there is the bizarre sight of her covetously caressing the blade of Hindley's knife-cum-pistol, meditating 'how powerful I should be possessing such an instrument!' (p. 140). But as Heathcliff comes to suggest, her strangely swift acceptance of brutality represents an emergence of hidden values, the kind she revealed as a child in defence of her possessions when urging that the young Heathcliff be thrown in the cellar. From the culture of such as Isabella, from a hidden violence which shows as soon as it is scratched, Heathcliff has learnt how property is ultimately defended.

The episodes involving Lockwood and Heathcliff's dogs reverberate forwards in the text and backwards in the story to the episode of Catherine and Heathcliff as children spying on the inhabitants of Thrushcross Grange. Then, Isabella and Edgar fighting over a puppy – deanimated into an item of property, 'a heap of warm hair' (p. 46) – arouses the young Heathcliff's contempt: 'When would you catch me wishing to have what Catherine wanted? . . . I'd not exchange, for a thousand lives, my condition here, for Edgar Linton's at Thrushcross Grange' (p. 47). Not a thousand pounds, but a thousand lives; young Heathcliff recognises a currency of life. Indeed, the only use he can enthusiastically imagine for the Grange is as a high platform from which to launch Joseph, and as a convenient surface to be painted with Hindley's blood. Moreover, this Heathcliff pointedly mocks the landlord mentality with its sense of siege, its suspicions, its readiness to shoot and hang in defence of property, its reliance on appearance and social class as infallible indices of criminality. Owner, wife, children and servants at the Grange are all complicit:

> 'What prey, Robert?' hallooed Linton from the entrance.
> 'Skulker has caught a little girl, sir', he replied, 'and there's a lad here', he added, making a clutch at me, 'who looks an out-and-outer! Very like, the robbers were for putting them through the window, to open the doors to the gang after you were all asleep, that they might murder us at their ease. Hold your tongue, you foul-mouthed thief, you! you shall go to the gallows for this. Mr. Linton, sir, don't lay by your gun!'
> 'No, no, Robert!' said the old fool. 'The rascals knew that yesterday was my rent day . . . There, John, fasten the chain. Give Skulker some water, Jenny. To beard a magistrate in his strong-hold, and on the Sabbath too! . . . would it not be a kindness to the country to hang him at once, before he shows his nature in acts as well as features?'
> . . . Mrs. Linton placed her spectacles on her nose and raised her hands in horror. The cowardly children crept nearer also, Isabella lisping –
> 'Frightful thing! Put him in the cellar, papa. He's exactly like the son of the fortune-teller, that stole my tame pheasant.' (pp. 47–8)

Old Linton's blusterings reveal how patriotism and religion sustain property ownership within his ideology ('a kindness to the country . . . and on the Sabbath too!'). The owner reassures himself that (like his son Edgar after him) he conveniently doubles as magistrate (and within a system of law recognising far more capital offences in crimes against property than in crimes against the person). Beyond the bolts, the chains and the dogs, lie the remedies of gun and gallows to defend the rents against sons of fortune-tellers and other 'out-and-outers', extremes of force which domestically are recapitulated in the blows, thrashings and floggings with which virtually every master controls his house.

As young Heathcliff quickly learns, Cathy can enter the Grange (figuratively and literally) thanks to a deference to class (and in her case gender) on which we have seen Lockwood vainly depending: 'she was a young lady and they made a discrimination between her treatment and mine' (p. 49). The values of the Grange are pleasingly aestheticised in those delightful surfaces of gold, silver, crimson and crystal which overlie the foundations of ownership, and which are not easily resisted: the Cathy who returns is a changed person; even the young Heathcliff sends forth this world with sighing, 'ah! it was beautiful!' (p. 46), though part of his future enterprise will be to subvert such values, to put gold 'to the use of paving stones' and polish tin 'to ape a service of silver' (p. 219).

What certainly attracts Heathcliff, though, is property as personal space. Wuthering Heights is claustrophobic, not because of its relative size or inferiority of furnishing, but because of the oppressive presence of selfish authority – Hindley and Frances laughing and drinking before the fire, while the children read sermons and learn 'Scripture names' under Joseph's tutelage. Heathcliff finds Edgar and Isabella foolish in not appreciating freedom within a property space. The room is beautiful, but additionally the children have it to themselves: 'We should have thought ourselves in heaven! . . . We laughed outright at the petted things, we did despise them! When would you . . . find us by ourselves, seeking entertainment in yelling, and sobbing, and rolling on the ground, divided by the whole room?' (pp. 46–7). Hindley enjoys a 'paradise' (p. 19) by the hearth of Wuthering Heights – and even Joseph can enjoy 'a sort of elysium alone' there (p. 236). In their youth Cathy and Heathcliff console themselves with substitutes: the dairywoman's cloak which they 'appropriate' in order to 'have a scamper on the moors, under its shelter' (p. 20); the room-like space they improvise in the arch of a dresser with a pinafore to curtain off Frances and Hindley, 'as snug as our means allowed' (p. 19). But such measures, like day-long escapes to the moors, are only play solutions: eventually they must come home; the pinafore is torn down and ears are boxed.

Emily Brontë may have been quite familiar with siege mentality. Anecdote has it that every evening her father loaded his pistols and every morning, after another night spent secure from intruders, discharged his weapons from the house doorway. One of the few stories of Emily from a contemporary witness reports the Reverend Patrick Brontë instructing Emily in target practice with those pistols [Gérin, 1971, pp. 147–8]. Likely human targets must have been envisaged as burglars or a discontented lower class (Charlotte Brontë was to depict the siege of a house by Luddite workers in *Shirley*). Even Emily's beloved dog 'Keeper' may have earned some part of its living at Haworth Parsonage in the way Skulker and his pup, Juno, Gnasher, Wolf and Throttler do in *Wuthering Heights*. The anecdote concerning her firearm training constitutes no anomaly; it is best understood as an uneccentric instance of the measures thought appropriate in the family to maintain domestic and personal security against intrusion.

But with such fascinating tensions in her background as that between the poverty of her Irish ancestors and the acquired conservatism of her clergyman father, Emily's attitudes towards property, force and the underclass might well have been contradictory or in some state of suspension – most suited, perhaps, to exploration *as* dramatic tensions. For Heathcliff the 'houseless' stood simultaneously in the older branches of her own family tree, on the Liverpool docks as she wrote, and imaginatively in the line of aim of her father's pistol as she levelled it to fire.

Patriarchy and its Anxieties

Heathcliff's disruptive effect on family and property is established when Earnshaw's presents for his children are lost and broken; cuckoo-fashion, Heathcliff physically displaces them in Earnshaw's greatcoat. The children's reaction introduces Heathcliff to the web of property and passion in his new environment.

Earnshaw has undoubtedly shown charity; the Good Samaritan – an important emblem for the eighteenth and nineteenth centuries in celebrating (though at the same time prudently limiting) the extension of charity – ghosts through his rescuing Heathcliff. Indeed, perhaps imprudently, Earnshaw goes further than the Samaritan. The latter has an innkeeper lodge and tend the victim, and later takes the time to check on the patient and settle up; Earnshaw takes a morally more complex path:

> ... his money and time being both limited, he thought it better to take it home with him at once, than run into vain expences there; because he

was determined he would not leave it as he found it. (p. 35)

With the object of charity neither at arm's length, nor yet incorporated legally and ritually into the family, Earnshaw prepares an explosive mixture of the incorporated and the excluded, of those with name and expectations and those without.

The children's forbearance towards Heathcliff dissolves into Hindley's blubbering and Cathy's spitting. Theirs is a common enough childish disappointment – insignificant, except that it springs from a norm of expectation built upon confidence in parents as providers of necessities and of goods fostering cultural growth or personal fulfilment, say for Hindley in music through the fiddle, and for Cathy in horse-riding through the whip. But Heathcliff, the 'poor, fatherless child' (p. 36), adds another dimension to the human existences the text envisages, one (if still with desire) without expectation. Cathy and Hindley's 'normal' behaviour thus acquires relativity. Not overly wealthy, and lacking the Grange's style, Wuthering Heights is still one of the 'respectable houses' of the locality, and substantial enough to let land to tenant-farmers (p. 65); its very representativeness deepens the irony of Cathy and Hindley's disappointment being a luxury by Heathcliff's standards. Cathy and Hindley only seem spoiled once Heathcliff enters the frame; how much more 'petted' the Linton children appear with Heathcliff alongside Cathy watching them at the Grange. Heathcliff's presence also modifies Cathy's perspective: years later, married to Edgar, Cathy will declare that he and Isabella are 'spoiled children, and fancy the world was made for their accommodation' (pp. 97–8).

Purposely or not, Heathcliff disrupts the passage of the fiddle and the whip between parent and child. The children respond in kind, frustrating even those basic expectations Earnshaw first grants him. They exclude Heathcliff from their property space, from bed and even from their room. Nelly, similarly disappointed of her apples and pears, puts the child on the landing, 'hoping it might be gone on the morrow' (p. 35). This act of exclusion rebounds very precisely, for Nelly is herself 'sent out of the house', although returning in a few days, not believing her 'banishment perpetual' (p. 36).

Nelly can view her punishment lightly, but an unironised threat of exile, banishment, dispossession or exclusion is frequently a feature of the drama and rhetoric of *Wuthering Heights*. Here, without grounds for confidence, the experience of the urchin excluded from the children's room is very different from Nelly's; like the bewildered Lockwood in Heathcliff's house (a bitterly satisfying reversal for Heathcliff), the urchin Heathcliff, threatened with renewed exclusion, can on his first night in the Earnshaws' house 'only ramble about the steps and passages' (p. 26). The affair of the colts amplifies these ideas. At this point Heathcliff enjoys some influence at the Heights through Earnshaw's self-justifying favouritism; by corollary, Hindley has had his own confident expectations eroded. There is no discernible irony when Nelly records that 'the young master had learnt to regard his father as an *oppressor* rather than a friend, and Heathcliff as a *usurper* of his parent's affections and his privileges' (p. 36; my italics).

Heathcliff blackmails the colt out of Hindley, threatening to tell Earnshaw of Hindley's past violence – and of any further violence should Hindley offer it:

> 'Throw it', [Heathcliff] replied, standing still, 'and then I'll tell how you boasted that you would turn me out of doors as soon as he died, and see whether he will not turn you out directly.' (p. 37)

The 'boast', whether actually Hindley's or just Heathcliff's invention, sounds like Hindley's, and – in Hindley's mind – would be credible as such to his father. Risking and coolly accepting violence, Heathcliff outfaces Hindley, shrewdly gambling on Hindley's fear of violent retribution from Earnshaw, and on his growing insecurity. Interfering with the transmission of property between parent and child again (the colts are presents from Earnshaw), Heathcliff further engineers collapse in Hindley's construction of himself as heir, extracting from him a confession of powerlessness to sustain the role. With or without justification, Hindley cannot trust his father, and so delivers the psychological triumph to Heathcliff in their long-term power struggle. Heathcliff gets 'what he wanted' (p. 38), and more than just the colt. Hindley's surrender frustratedly turns to abuse as word-magic, and acknowledges Heathcliff's intervention between father and son, master and heir. Through most of this chapter Nelly refers to 'Hindley', but to 'the young master' when talking of Heathcliff as 'usurper'. Here Hindley is 'young Earnshaw' again, stressing his immediately vulnerable role:

> 'Take my colt, gipsy, then!' said young Earnshaw. 'And I pray that he may break your neck; take him, and be damned, you beggarly interloper! and wheedle my father out of all he has – only, afterwards, show him what you are, imp of Satan.' (p. 38)

Crucially, Heathcliff focuses their conflict down to threats of mutual expulsion. Hindley will not risk being 'turned out of doors', for the other side of siege mentality is fear of houselessness: fear of invasion, of intrusion, is complemented by fear of ejection and exclusion. Often this is the threat in *Wuthering Heights*, the nightmare of its most intense moments – a figure in the snow banging for entry at a locked door; a child in the storm rapping at a closed window. Barriers between rooms and between the inside and outside of houses, with characters positioned on opposite sides, prove recurrent foci of dramatic tension. Characters are locked in or out, thrown in or out, their entry or exit barred; they must break in or out, spy, or communicate surreptitiously.

Once Hindley inherits the Heights, he consolidates power by defining his and others' spaces. Joseph and Nelly must keep to the back-kitchen, and while Hindley insists on the 'house' for himself, Heathcliff's spatial and cultural exclusion proceeds apace:

> He drove him from their company to the servants, deprived him of the instructions of the curate, and insisted that he should labour out of doors instead. (p. 44)

Peer pressure legitimises Hindley's actions: from Old Linton's stoutly orthodox perspective, a girl of Cathy's class and age should be removed from the influence of that 'little Lascar, or ... American or Spanish castaway' (p. 48); reinforcing the social and cultural gulf between them is only proper. Old Linton's re-education of Hindley even runs to supplying him with a son of that very Skulker loosed upon Heathcliff and Cathy. Cheered by the obvious deterioration of Heathcliff and the contrasting refinement of Cathy during her period at the Grange, Hindley complacently ventures to reduce their attachment to an occasional handshake between servant and gentlewoman.

Admitted to the Grange, Cathy succumbs to the graces of an environment displaying orthodox values in visual style. She is caused to recognise a cultural gulf between her conformist self and Heathcliff, between her potential destiny and his. But Heathcliff also falls towards conformism. He watches the new ladylike Cathy with 'shame and pride' (p. 52). If he could reject the Thrushcross Grange of Edgar and Isabella with exuberance, only augmenting his sense of his own worth, he cannot so easily dismiss the Grange-formed Cathy. A shrill pride dominates when he reacts to her concern for her dress: 'I shall be as dirty as I please, and I like to be dirty, and I will be dirty' (p. 53). But Heathcliff's only other recourse, if he is to compete for Cathy, is provisionally to accept those standards which also compel his shame:

> Nelly, make me decent, I'm going to be good . . . I wish I had light hair and a fair skin, and was dressed and behaved as well, and had a chance of being as rich as he will be. (p. 55)

Cathy, he fears, may be moving through style beyond him, and certainly she will shortly complain of his society as 'no company at all, when people know nothing and say nothing' (p. 69). Yet Wuthering Heights offers him no springboard from which to challenge the culture of Thrushcross Grange for Cathy on *its* terms. Indeed Heathcliff swings into an adolescent spiral of negation in which he derives perverse satisfaction from pre-empting Hindley's degradations through self-brutalisation.

The best opportunity for revenge – Hindley's dropping Hareton – Heathcliff mismanages by instinctively catching the child. Hindley is saved suffering and Hareton survives as heir, making so deeply ironic Heathcliff's acting as 'the instrument of thwarting his own revenge' (p. 74). Hindley, however, as his drunken outpourings reveal, incarnates the anxieties of patriarchy. Nelly's precaution of 'stowing his son away in the kitchen cupboard' provokes Hindley's conclusion 'you've sworn between you to murder that child!', a paranoid suspicion ironically undercut not only by Nelly's concern to protect the child from his father, but by Hindley's subsequent jeopardising of Hareton's life and Heathcliff's saving it. With Frances dead, and Hareton likely to remain his only child, Hindley is deeply insecure about his own role as master, his son's as heir, and about his masculinity. (He does not mention Frances, but his boast that he has 'just crammed Kenneth, head-downmost, in the Blackhorse marsh' is an angry fantasy of punishment deflected onto the doctor who had so bluntly predicted her death.) The drunken Hindley easily slips into Old Linton's tones, loudly asserting that very position and those powers his insecure self finds so precarious. His stance of the free-born Englishman enjoying authority and liberty of action – 'No law in England can hinder a man from keeping his house decent' (p. 73) – rapidly mutates into the squalid and self-defeating variant of 'I wouldn't murder you [Heathcliff] to-night, unless, perhaps, I set the house on fire: but that's as my fancy goes' (p. 75). Towards Hareton he fluctuates between showing a 'wild-beast's fondness' and a 'madman's rage', unable to trust his son and heir's affection (any more than he had trusted his own father), and writhing in the possibilities of the son turning into an 'unnatural cub' (p. 73) – 'By God, as if I would rear such a monster!' (p. 74) – and of himself proving a worthless father: 'Any one will do better for him than I shall' (p. 75). Heathcliff's recognition of how saving Hareton has lost him the chance to explode Hindley's uncomfortably worn patriarchal stance is tellingly phrased:

> A miser who has parted with a lucky lottery ticket for five shillings and finds next day he has lost in the bargain five thousand pounds, could not show a blanker countenance. (p. 74)

Heathcliff's departure is triggered by more than his hearing of Cathy's acceptance of Edgar in marriage. The episode is highly theatrical, with Cathy unaware of Heathcliff listening or of his leaving at a crucial transition in her remarks – just as she declares that 'it would degrade me to marry Heathcliff now' (p. 80), but also in the very breath before she adds that he will never know how much she loves him. Heathcliff has gone when Cathy indignantly asserts that marrying Edgar will not entail separation from Heathcliff; he has gone when she explains that if she and Heathcliff married they would be beggars, and that her best motive for marrying Edgar is her intention of using her position to help Heathcliff rise and escape Hindley's power. Significantly, Heathcliff does remain after she has explained that she loves Edgar 'because he will be rich, and I shall like to be the greatest woman of the neighbourhood, and I shall be proud of having such a husband' (p. 78). However, her explaining how Hindley's actions have influenced her decision is crucial:

> I've no more business to marry Edgar Linton than I have to be in heaven; and if the wicked man in there had not brought Heathcliff so low, I shouldn't have thought of it. (p. 80)

Traditionally critics have emphasised the first part of this remark; rarely the second. Heathcliff's agony hinges on the role of his old enemy Hindley's actions. What the drama dictates that Heathcliff *does not* hear, intensifies the cruelty of the explanation he does hear. He leaves having had his dream of revenge upon Hindley ludicrously undercut by his 'good turn' (p. 87) in saving Hareton. He leaves knowing that pre-empting Hindley's persecution by cultivating a self-willed 'impression of inward and outward repulsiveness' (p. 67) has utterly misfired, transforming him in the new Cathy's eyes from the obvious prospect as a husband to an impossible one. But he may also be understood as leaving in search of a common remedy to his various frustrations: revenge on Hindley may not be separate from the problem of his own relation to society and its benefits, or from the now central issue of retrieving his relationship with Cathy. When he returns he has cultivated differences in himself to those specific ends. To Cathy he will say, 'I struggled only for you' (p. 96) – but that is to struggle with his whole condition of exclusion.

Having once been driven to and beyond the margins of community, Heathcliff's return becomes a second arrival, reworking on altered terms those collisions with property-culture in which his relationship with Cathy has become so deeply enmeshed.

At the Grange he meets familiar tactics. If Nelly avoids issues of status by talking of 'That Heathcliff . . . who used to live at Mr. Earnshaw's', Edgar promptly glosses 'Heathcliff' as 'the gipsy – the ploughboy' (p. 94) and, like Hindley, sets about assigning people to appropriate and controllable spaces; in particular, Heathcliff to the kitchen. In Edgar's view, Heathcliff will have 'a long walk, wherever he may lodge tonight' (p. 96). But Cathy slices through Edgar's disposals of space with mockery: Edgar and Isabella, she proposes, must sit at one table, being gentry, and she and Heathcliff at another, 'being of the lower orders' (p. 95).

Edgar's stake in decorum jeopardised by Cathy's 'welcoming a runaway servant as a brother' (p. 95), extends beyond master-household relationships to his marriage, founded as it is in the ideology of property and its expression in style. Yet, paradoxically, this also commits Edgar to recognising Heathcliff's newly acquired facility with the language, gestures and customs of the owning class. As Cathy quite plausibly urges Edgar, Heathcliff is 'now worthy of any one's regard, and it would honour the first gentleman in the country to be his friend' (p. 98). Yet Heathcliff's manners are principally the means enabling him to engage with society on a level footing, and in turn to pursue revenge by subverting the very social forms and structures previously used to exclude him.

Heathcliff's paying Hindley liberal rent for lodging at the Heights initially seems ironic at Heathcliff's expense. But this is the beginning of Heathcliff's gambling his way to becoming mortgagee of the Heights, reversing the ironies as Hindley commits the traditional cardinal sin of the landowner – borrowing money against land. Hindley is thus eventually dispossessed of that very property which had empowered him to engineer the young Heathcliff's exclusion. It is more sweet a revenge than Heathcliff's initial intention of glimpsing Cathy once more and then simply killing Hindley and himself, and more than a personal revenge. Joseph's diction (which denotes individuals in terms of family relationships) intimates that Heathcliff is undermining the structures of family and inheritance themselves: 'I'course, he tells Dame Catherine hah hor father's goold runs intuh his pocket, and her father's son gallops dahn t'Broad road, while he flees afore to oppen t'pikes?' (p. 104).

Seeking revenge, but with no single plan, Heathcliff becomes a chess-player developing different areas of the board. Advancing boldly, he is careful to observe the rules of the society he is set on dismantling. Isabella speaks of his 'diabolical prudence' (p. 152) – and Heathcliff congratulates himself on keeping 'strictly within the limits of the law' (p. 151).

Isabella's infatuation presents another property as prize – one he considers pursuable without harming Cathy's interests, for engineering his possession of Thrushcross Grange could only result in Cathy enjoying the property more fully through him than she does as Edgar's wife. (By contrast, Heathcliff refuses Isabella any part in ownership at the Heights.)

The elopement also highlights his argument with Cathy. Cathy and Heathcliff's antagonism, co-existing with their love, receives little explicit expression until Heathcliff contrives to see Cathy in her illness: '*Why* did you despise me? *Why* did you betray your own heart, Cathy?' (p. 161). Cathy's marriage constitutes the greatest barrier between them, and her acceptance of that marriage, which Heathcliff frustratedly respects, makes the barrier self-enforced and to that extent the more frustrating. Heathcliff's reproach is evident when he counters Cathy's suggestion that he has not thought of her during his absence with the rejoinder that her marriage implies she has thought of him much less. Reproach lies in his bitter rejection of Cathy's right to intervene in his courting Isabella, seeing that Cathy has already spurned him as a husband. However, Cathy's measured willingness actually to contemplate Isabella and Heathcliff's marriage provokes his strongest words:

> Having levelled my palace, don't erect a hovel and complacently admire your own charity in giving me that for a home. If I imagined you really wished me to marry Isabella, I'd cut my throat!' (p. 112)

Laying siege to the Heights, and angling for some purchase on Thrushcross Grange, Heathcliff's actions and metaphors here interlock: Cathy's marriage has destroyed his dream of a 'palace' of fulfilled love; seriously to be offered Isabella as a wife by Cathy is to be offered a 'hovel' for that promised palace, to be patronised emotionally in a way which echoes the economic patronage of an owning class's charity.

Marrying Isabella also cold-bloodedly prostitutes that institution of marriage which has separated him from Cathy, creating through the sister a black parody of Cathy's marriage to the brother, a self-mutilation perversely designed to impress

Cathy with its painfulness. Heathcliff may not respond immediately to Cathy's insensitive prediction of her bearing Edgar half-a-dozen sons, but there is a bitter riposte in Heathcliff's later telling Nelly that he has 'avoided, up to this period, giving [his wife Isabella] the slightest right to claim a separation' (p. 151): Isabella's tears on 'the very morrow of our wedding' (p. 150), together with her questions and laboured reticences in her letter to Nelly, indicate that Heathcliff's care for the completeness of his travesty has only spurred him on to its sexual consummation.

In the later days of his plotting Heathcliff speaks far more openly about his purposes to Nelly:

> 'My son is prospective owner of your place, and I should not wish him to die till I was certain of being his successor. Besides, he's *mine*, and I want the triumph of seeing *my* descendant faily lord of their estates; my child hiring their children, to till their father's lands for wages – That is the sole consideration which can make me endure the whelp.' (p. 208)

His forcibly pressurising Catherine and Linton into marriage further exemplifies his determination to transform marriage and inheritance from instruments of his exclusion into the tools of his revenge. Yet as symmetry of revenge forms under his hands and through the years, Heathcliff risks becoming the arch-defender of patriarchy. He has deconstructed and subverted marriage and inheritance as foundations of property ownership, yet drives towards a grotesque mimicry and extension rather than alteration of the systems he attacks, at a cost that includes the distortion of others and of himself and his son – who *is* his own son as well as a Linton. Being prepared to risk condemning the future to experiencing Linton as landlord – a manufactured monster of greed with only a poisoned appreciation of what might link man and wife, child and parent – constitutes a terrible legacy.

After Edgar's death, Heathcliff enters the Grange with 'no ceremony of knocking, or announcing his name; he was master, and availed himself of the master's privilege to walk straight in' (p. 286). The nameless man has trodden a spiral – has left behind the namelessness of exclusion and even the inhibiting paradoxes of his acquired name, and through the power of possession has at last entered into a new namelessness, that of the master who does not require to be announced. With Linton's death Heathcliff sweeps every last remaining chip on the table into his lap. There remains his persecution of the dispossessed, Hareton and Catherine, as proxy victims, but this attenuated phase of his revenge falters. Having followed through his revenge on those most closely involved with him, on Earnshaws and Lintons, on Hindley, on Edgar, on Isabella – and arguably even on Cathy, he visits the sins of the fathers on the children; and in doing so the revenger in one generation becomes the tyrant of another.

The Divided Woman

The editorial consciousness at the outer rim of the illusion of *Wuthering Heights* is presented as male. Dates heading passages belong to Lockwood's life; the story is begun, interrupted and continued as *his* moods, wishes, journeys and health determine; it is he who requires that Nelly abbreviate nothing, he who at another point decides to condense her words. Lockwood, however, observes relatively little directly apart from his own visits to the Heights, and those episodes reveal the unreliability of his judgement – especially where his own masculinity is involved. (Indeed, his tendencies towards dizziness and fainting imply a wry version of stereotypes of the weak woman.) He is a more appropriate listener than narrator, the sick little boy to be entertained in bed with a nurse's tale designed to correct his perceptions. Jacobs persuasively sees Emily Brontë using Lockwood in a 'satirical miming and disempowering of male authority', seeking 'to appropriate and delegitimise [man's] power, before telling [her] anti-patriarchal truths' [p. 205].

It is women who dominate narration, controlling thereby the selection of events and propositions about their interpretation – mainly Nelly, but also Zillah, Catherine, Isabella through her letter, and Cathy through her diary. Writing as 'Ellis Bell', in engagement with male-dominated cultural institutions, Emily Brontë turns to narrators echoing her own activity as woman-writer. In patriarchal society, private narration can offer women a consoling control over events: Cathy's desolation under Hindley's regime is confided to her diary; Isabella's sufferings in marriage are given epistolary form. In this novel such writing escapes from the margins of society and authorship, as does Emily's novel. Not, of course, that female narrators enjoy any immunity from criticism: men (such as Heathcliff), as well as women, are victims of patriarchy; women (such as Nelly) are also complicit in it. (See the third section of the 'Survey'.)

Marginalised as narrators, male characters such as Edgar, Hindley, Linton and Hareton in consequence command less reader sympathy. (Linton does write and narrate, but only to betray his utter subjection to the later Heathcliff.) Heathcliff is in comparison accorded privileged modes of expressing his consciousness. These include oral narration (the visit to Thrushcross Grange and his dealings with Cathy's grave), heightened language, and a capacity to soliloquise – or to speak with a freedom which ignores others' presence:

> I have no pity! I have no pity! The worms writhe, the more I yearn to crush out their entrails! It is a moral teething, and I grind with greater energy, in proportion to the increase of pain. (p. 152)

Diaries have been recognised as especially important in offering women laboratories of experience and interpretation unsupervised by male authority. The presentation of Cathy's diary allows such a consciousness to be shared. Technically, Lockwood mediates the diary, but he records it as he would an architectural inscription, and the reader has no fears of distortion. Private diaries automatically connote authenticity; here lies an 'unknown Catherine' to be 'deciphered' by the reader through her 'faded hieroglyphics' as much as by Lockwood (p. 18).

Cathy's essential spirit shows in her writing in the margins and blanks of printed books, undermining the authority of the printed words of others and prioritising her purposes of self-definition [*cf.* Musselwhite]. Her secret text declares a rebellion which finds expression when she and Heathcliff tear up their imposed, oppressive and joyless Sunday texts; it ends with her anguish at Hindley punitively separating her from Heathcliff. Divided from Heathcliff, Cathy's secret text of selfhood lapses.

The episode of Lockwood's dreams works to marshal

sympathy with the diarist. In the light of the violent piety of the dream-Joseph, of the chapel-folk and the fiercely evangelical Jabes Branderham, the justness of the diarist's rebellion against the oppression of a domestic regime legitimised by just such religious enthusiasm is clear. Moreover, Cathy is associated with the lost and freezing dream-child with her 'little, ice-cold hand' and 'feeble scratching', the 'waif' (pp. 23–4) begging for entry who is cruelly shunned by Lockwood both in dreaming and waking. His attitudes alienate the reader while the emotional force of Heathcliff's crying 'Come in, come in!' (p. 27) wins through. In these pages Cathy is an absent centre of event and feeling, firmly claiming the reader's sympathies.

As the female child, Cathy lacks the heir's burden of expectation which crushes Hindley and which automatically defines the antagonism between himself and the excluded Heathcliff. By corollary, Heathcliff is Cathy's natural ally, for by gender she also has little to expect from inheritance. In time the falsely reassuring equilibrium between male and female in childhood (a fiddle for Hindley, a whip for Cathy; a ball marked 'H' and a ball marked 'C'), and between incorporated and excluded male (a colt for Hindley and a colt for Heathcliff), is uncompromisingly replaced by Hindley's mastery, under which *both* Heathcliff and Cathy 'promised fair to grow up as rude as savages' (p. 44). Cathy's life is preshaped by the patriarchal matrix, and her marginalisation by gender echoes Heathcliff's marginalisation by class: 'My great miseries in this world have been Heathcliff's miseries, and I watched and felt each from the beginning' [p. 103]. To some degree Heathcliff and Cathy's recognition of themselves in each other, their sense of co-identity or mutual alterity – 'Nelly, I *am* Heathcliff' (p. 82); 'I *cannot* live without my life! I *cannot* live without my soul!' (p. 167) – is grounded in a lived social identity defined by the structures of family, gender and inheritance.

Marriage, however, does provide for the woman. The woman's long-term means of life are bound up in marriage and child-bearing, where man is, in Lockwood's words, the 'favoured possessor' and woman the 'beneficent fairy' (p. 12). Here the man may be able to overlook a wife's lack of name and money without immediate disaster, as Hindley does in marrying Frances, but the woman faces other consequences in doing the same in choosing a husband. (Edgar cannot disinherit Isabella, but he does disown her.) Lockwood can even manage without marrying at all, despite occasional impulses to flirt: duty towards the idea of marriage so done, he can, as a man, survive outside the institution, apparently somewhat relieved, returning instead to the arms of the busy world.

When Cathy is injured by Skulker, Mrs Linton recognises both the moral and physical damage that the girl's marriage prospects may have incurred through Cathy 'scouring the country with a gipsy' and the fact 'she may be lamed for life!' (p. 48). Recovering Cathy's potential role as wife begins with a class and fertility ritual in which all at the Grange are individually and corporately involved, a passive robing and annointing before the future husband:

> She sat on the sofa quietly. Mrs Linton took off the grey cloak of the dairymaid which we had borrowed for our excursion, shaking her head and expostulating with her. . . . Then the woman-servant brought a basin of warm-water, and washed her feet; and Mr Linton made a tumbler of negus, and Isabella emptied a plateful of cakes into her lap, and Edgar stood gaping at a distance. Afterwards, they dried and combed her beautiful hair, and gave her a pair of enormous slippers, and wheeled her to the fire. (p. 49)

Here commences Cathy's sense of division, coinciding, the ritual suggests, with puberty. Heathcliff and childhood are on one side, Edgar and the structured concerns of adult life on the other. It is a passage she never completes, being instead 'led to adopt a double character without exactly intending to deceive anyone' (p. 66). Cathy enters a socially induced schizophrenia as a consequence of the contradictory demands she recognises. She is thrown into trying to satisfy the expectations of both Heathcliff and Edgar, as well as her own feelings towards the pair of them. Nelly has 'many a laugh at her perplexities and untold troubles, which she vainly strove to hide' (p. 67), but the reader can trace the pain of Cathy's perplexity.

Cathy finds herself in a spiral of contradiction not out of pride or selfishness or treachery, but from trying to sustain simultaneously her long-standing emotional commitment to

Heathcliff, *and* the role her class and gender determine for her, and which – while not cancelling out her feelings for Heathcliff – seems just as normal and necessary to her, and allows, indeed encourages her, also to love Edgar. She believes, and believes it reasonable to believe, that she can have both marriage and Heathcliff. As her scratchings on the window-ledge intimate, she finds it impossible to view her future without marriage; but it also becomes problematic for her to relate her deepest passion, Heathcliff himself, to marriage as her ideology constructs it. Only in understanding this mental state does such a sentiment of hers as 'if Heathcliff and I married, we should be beggars' (p. 81) rise above pettiness and achieve the force of reason. Her perplexity is expressed in her persistent postulation of a way of living in which those contradictions in her feelings and allegiances which Nelly perceives will not prove contradictory at all. Nelly concludes that in expecting to maintain a close relationship with Heathcliff while married to Edgar, Cathy is either ignorant of her duties or 'a wicked unprincipled girl' (p. 82). Yet Cathy acts in good faith; she cannot see she might be using Edgar – and indeed Nelly has to admit that Cathy is 'over-fond' (p. 91) of him. But the moment Heathcliff returns, she attempts to live out that state of contradiction. Her joy at Heathcliff's reappearance issues in the paradox of her embracing and squeezing *Edgar*.

Cathy is thus on a tightrope which Edgar and Heathcliff are both vibrating. Heathcliff returns aggrieved at her marriage and seeking revenge; Edgar's indignation at her entertaining Heathcliff finally breaks out. Cathy is amazed to find herself in the middle; frustrated by Heathcliff's animosity on the one side and Edgar's 'unreasonable tone of displeasure' on the other, she addresses her self-justification more to the heavens than to either of them:

> 'I'm delightfully rewarded for my kindness to each! After constant indulgence of one's weak nature, and the other's bad one, I earn, for thanks, two samples of blind ingratitude, stupid to absurdity! (p. 115)

For Edgar, Cathy is 'absurd' in her welcome for Heathcliff; for Cathy, both Heathcliff and Edgar are 'absurd' in finding fault with her: to Nelly she observes, in perfect innocence,

'You are aware I am no way blameable in this matter'.

Surrounded with irreconcilable demands, Cathy retreats into illness – at first, consciously and manipulatively. She tells Nelly to inform Edgar 'that I'm in danger of being seriously ill – I wish it may prove true' (p. 116). The masquerade becomes 'a brain fever' for male medicine. But Cathy's illness is a specifically female, anorexic response to the paradoxes imposed on her in a male-authored society. Trapped, and ironically in search of 'a chance of life', she unveils the space of illness into which movement is possible when, in the world of health, oscillating between Heathcliff and Edgar, she can move nowhere without frustration. In her wanderings she seeks the release of other free spaces: 'I wish I were out of doors! I wish I were a girl again' (p. 126). She improvises substitute rooms and homes, fantasising her bed as 'the fairy cave under Peniston Crag' (p. 123), and she grasps at states of happiness and resolution associated with the past of her childhood at the Heights and with death. She wishes she were 'in my own bed in the old house' (p. 124), and to Nelly she recounts a delusion of being 'in the oak-panelled bed at home'. Rationalising the misery she feels after Edgar and Heathcliff's fight, she actually thinks herself a child again, and her misery a consequence of 'the separation that Hindley had ordered between me and Heathcliff' and of her thereby being 'laid alone, for the first time' (p. 125). It is a telling delusion, linking her past exclusion from Heathcliff at the hands of an authority-figure within structures of inheritance, to her current exclusion from him by an authority-figure within the institution of marriage: Edgar has 'absolutely *required*' her to recognise the impossibility of being his friend and Heathcliff's and to 'choose' between them (p. 118). She also recounts suddenly being recalled to the present while so vividly revisiting her past at the Heights:

> Supposing at twelve years old I had been wrenched from the Heights, and every early association, and my all in all, as Heathcliff was at that time, and been converted at a stroke into Mrs. Linton, the lady of Thrushcross Grange, and the wife of a stranger; an exile, and outcast, thenceforth, from what had been my world – You may fancy a glimpse of the abyss where I grovelled! (p. 142)

Cathy's intense sensations of an abyss of exclusion link her in suffering with Heathcliff. She proceeds to musing on her 'narrow home out yonder', an idea which grotesquely mutates from the shape of the oak-panelled bed to the shape of her imagined coffin – significantly lying not with the Lintons under the chapel roof but, freed from allegiance to houses (in the sense of both buildings and family), 'in the open air' (p. 128). Beyond illness, death itself is opened up as the space of resolution. Cathy moves into delirium in response to a world which for her is itself insanely unheeding of what is perfectly sane. Ophelia-like, she experiences cryptic gleams of insight into Heathcliff's behaviour and, indeed, Nelly's. But her failure to recognise her own reflection disturbingly indicates how far she is travelling from an insupportable existence, and expresses what Grove calls the 'ideology of what is "true" to women . . . the experience of being coincident, divided, implausible' [1986, p. 72].

After Cathy's death, Nelly leaves a window open for Heathcliff to enter and see Cathy's body. On returning Nelly finds a curl of light-coloured hair on the floor – plainly Edgar's – and that Heathcliff has substituted for it, in a locket around Cathy's neck, a lock of his own. Nelly replaces the two, twisted together. So Cathy goes to the grave not with Edgar's lock alone (as Edgar would wish), or with Heathcliff's alone (as Heathcliff wishes), but with them twisted into an emblem of the paradox that has driven her there.

To see Cathy's tragedy requires seeing her as more than a selfish, shallow, wilful woman – 'fierce, faithless and foolish' for one Edwardian critic – who marries the wrong man for vain reasons and then insists on having the best of both worlds – destroying herself out of petulance when she cannot. It helps to ask why, when Heathcliff returns transformed, Emily Brontë does not have the two of them run off adulterously? The energy and resourcefulness of both Heathcliff and Cathy would guarantee the credibility of such an action, but ideological constraints bind the characters just as much as does their passion. Even Heathcliff does not so much as suggest their running away – although he has no qualms about eloping with Isabella, about kidnapping, or about flirting with murder and suicide. Cathy (and Heathcliff for her sake) accepts the claims of marriage at the same time as insisting upon the integrity of her passion. Marriage cannot be blithely ignored or unwritten in the cause of even their immortal love. With that acceptance there is the anguish of paradox for Cathy, for Heathcliff, and indeed for Edgar Linton. Cathy is a woman divided between her right to passion and the only viable mode of life and feeling within the horizons of her class and gender. Understanding the monumentality of marriage within nineteenth-century ideology [see Calder] (and it may well require an effort of imagination in a post-permissive, serial-marriage society) is essential to understanding the novel's terms of dramatic paradox.

Unquiet Slumbers: Ghosts and Literacy

Wuthering Heights teems with references to ghosts and hauntings. However, many dissolve at a touch. When Nelly sees 'something white moving irregularly, evidently by another agent than the wind', the apparition is not 'a creature of the other world' but Isabella's dog, trussed up by Heathcliff (p. 129). The face Cathy sees in her illness ('Oh! Nelly, the room is haunted') resolves into her own reflection (p. 123).

In some texts ghosts do have a dramatic presence, interacting with characters, affecting the development and meaning of events. What can be agreed about *Wuthering Heights* is that *belief* in ghosts, as evident in both rural and urban eighteenth-century England, has a vital dramatic function. The presence of belief, however, need not imply the phenomena themselves.

Heathcliff and Cathy's childhood bonding is strengthened in Gimmerton kirkyard: Cathy recalls, 'We've braved its ghosts often together, and dared each other to stand among the graves and ask them to come' (p. 126). Such memories fuel Cathy's solution to being separated from Heathcliff, fostering the idea of their sharing a life in death. To Heathcliff she declares that should he feel distress at anything she has said in life, so will she also feel distress in her grave. Heathcliff's outburst following her death demands that her ghost walk:

> And I pray one prayer – I repeat it till my tongue stiffens – Catherine Earnshaw, may you not rest, as long as I am living! You said I killed you – haunt me, then! The murdered *do* haunt their murderers. I believe – I know that ghosts *have* wandered on earth. Be with me always – take

any form – drive me mad! only *do* not leave me in this abyss, where I cannot find you! (p. 167)

Cathy may have absorbed such beliefs in childhood; her words to Heathcliff echo Nelly's traditional song to the infant Hareton, 'It was far in the night, and the bairnies grat/The mither beneath the mools heard that' (p. 76). The readiness of her superstitious reaction to her own reflection suggests those beliefs persist into adulthood. Indeed, unless this is understood to be so, her most intense scene with Heathcliff risks collapsing into cruel trickery with metaphors.

Heathcliff certainly believes in ghosts. In his bereavement he needs that belief to explain his sense of Cathy's continuing presence; moreover, a state of being beyond life, yet neither in Heaven nor Hell, offers a transcendental space for that exclusive love with Cathy which the constraints of life forbid. Their love causes both Cathy and Heathcliff to reject the traditional Heaven, as in Cathy's dream where Heaven does not seem to be her home and she is flung out onto the moors to wake sobbing for joy. Heathcliff's bald directions for his funeral involve no religious service; having nearly attained *his* heaven, he has no wish for anyone else's. Heathcliff must contrive some private space where Cathy is unannihilated, not as a saint in Nelly's Christian Heaven, but in an existence promising some substitute for the relationship denied them. 'The spectre of a hope' (p. 291) by which he lives is in fact his hope of the spectral.

Heathcliff's desires have a quality of blackness, inversion, perversity. That perversity, however, his wanting to be haunted – and in any form, his insistence upon death as life, charts the scale of his anguish. While to Cathy's face he may fervently deny the charge of his killing her, with her death he embraces the terrible idea to strengthen his hope of being haunted by her. Towards the end of his life Heathcliff certainly believes that he is seeing Cathy's ghost, relentlessly drawing him on to the grave and on to that bizarre, tragically or pathetically constructed freedom with her.

The characters themselves are divided on the subject. Heathcliff warns Nelly that her disobedience will 'prove, practically, that the dead are not annihilated' (p. 334), producing a very different atmosphere from Catherine taunting

Joseph and Hareton with future hauntings. Heathcliff is serious; Catherine, frequently dubbed 'witch' by superstitious characters, satirises Joseph and Hareton's credulity. The novel embodies an opposition – and an unmistakably nineteenth-century one – of superstition versus a broadly-based literacy. Hareton eventually passes from the one state to the other. But such passages are not easy, for Emily Brontë records a lived tension in the history of British culture, finding its expression in the uncertainties, the fears and desires of individual lives. Yet although the novel, together with its audience, is necessarily part of a culture of literacy, it cannot wholly explode the idea of ghosts; without some possibility, without belief having respectability, Heathcliff's desires and actions could only appear ludicrous. Nevertheless, ultimate explanations of events and behaviour in physical and psychological terms are sufficient, and in some ways much more compelling.

Limited to holding and kissing Cathy while she is dying and when she is dead, it is not surprising if Heathcliff's imagination turns gothically morbid, excavating Cathy's coffin the evening of her burial, having the sexton open it when Edgar is buried and making arrangements for his own and Cathy's coffins to lie open alongside one another. His healthy emotions of love have been thwarted by social constraints and turned back into the only channel, rational or irrational, left to him. So he reworks the negation of death into a landscape of fulfilment. Social constraints still hamper him: suicide will not accelerate a union with Cathy for convention dictates the suicide's burial in unhallowed ground, and not, as Heathcliff plans, in an embrace of physical decay with Cathy. So, like Cathy, he eventually half-wills his own decline ambiguously. For the traditionally perceived Byronic superman this is a remarkably female solution, to be seen specifically as the creation of the woman writer.

The extremes to which Heathcliff goes, and his extraordinary final goal, need not turn his relationship with Cathy into a mystical, symbolic or allegorical statement. If Cathy the woman says 'Nelly, I *am* Heathcliff', this is her struggle with language to express the intensity of her human love for Heathcliff – not a theological statement about the relationship of their souls in a pre-existence. As Moody argues, the novel does not present 'an alien *sort* of passion [and] a duration and intensity quite outside normal experience' [p. 28], and such judgements only diminish the judges. It presents an eighteenth-century man and woman seeking a space for love beyond death within a framework of belief which their own culture did not discount, and driven to do so by historically specific social forces.

The narrative structure makes the question of whether Heathcliff and Cathy achieve their goal unanswerable. No narrator has the authority to judge. Readers who view death as annihilation will, with a greater indignation about the paradoxes Cathy and Heathcliff face, appreciate the defiance and energy of their struggle towards their imagined heaven. Readers disposed to believe with them that they do succeed, have many images to carry away – of Cathy sobbing for joy at being ejected from Heaven; of ghostly figures at the window at the Heights, near the church, and on the moors. Nelly herself believes, with most of her orthodoxly Christian mind, that 'the dead are at peace' (p. 337); she hopes that the 'landlord', now the 'tenant' of the grave, sleeps as soundly as she assumes Cathy and Edgar do. Lockwood leaves, taking a last view of the three graves, each at different stages of being covered by vegetation:

> I lingered round them, under that benign sky; watched the moths fluttering among the heath, and hare-bells, listened to the soft wind breathing through the grass; and wondered how anyone could ever imagine unquiet slumbers for the sleepers in that quiet earth. (p. 338)

Yet Lockwood is not the final interpreter. His sentiments blend with the benign sky and season and rhythmically consititute a gesture of closure, but the novel has shown other skies, other winds. Besides, other perspectives on Cathy and Heathcliff are provided through Hareton and Catherine.

In Hareton and Catherine's story, the social perspective is in higher relief, and problematically so for the reader without any such perspective on Heathcliff and Cathy. As Buchen indicates, if Heathcliff and Cathy's story is viewed as 'a typical romantic novel' then Hareton and Catherine's is bound to appear 'a respectable Victorian novel', thus producing 'Brontë the schizophrenic novelist' [p. 16].

Heathcliff's movement from persecuting Hareton and Catherine to becoming preoccupied with rejoining Cathy, is accelerated when he finds Catherine teaching Hareton to read a book she has given him:

> 'It is a poor conclusion, is it not?' he observed, having brooded a while on the scene he had just witnessed. 'An absurd termination to my violent exertions?' (p. 323)

As Hindley confirmed Heathcliff's exclusion from the owning class by cultural degradation, so Heathcliff has used it in revenge against Hareton, and even against Catherine. He succeeds to the extent that Hareton's illiteracy divides him from Catherine at the moment when she and Linton are actually bonding through the giving and sharing of books. Characters are seen in differing relations to books [*cf*., MacKibben; Musselwhite]. Edgar (at one point to Cathy's fury) has his library; Heathcliff gives up book-learning in his adolescence. Lockwood tries to bar the dream-Cathy's entry with books. Catherine and Joseph threaten each other's library – though Joseph's extends little beyond the Bible on which he counts his money and the tracts with which he has made others' lives a misery. In this context, Catherine mocks Joseph's superstition very pointedly by pretending that one of hers is a book of spells. That Catherine is able to protect her own literacy at the Heights, and then resocialise Hareton through literacy, constitutes a powerful undermining of Heathcliff's strategies. This shared literacy becomes the central motif of the new Wuthering Heights.

In the nineteenth century literacy could appear as the key to resolving class problems. A burgeoning urban and industrial working class threatened the dominant classes with actual and potential claims upon political power and cultural institutions. The spread of literacy among working people aided the growth of class-consciousness, so management of that literacy from above was essential for the dominant classes. 'Educating our masters', ensuring that literacy involved a sharing of dominant values among the newly literate rather than an oppositional culture, became the project. The manipulative edge of this process, however, was masked both by the sincerity of motives among the reformers involved and by the fact of literacy undeniably bringing reward to the newly literate. What was read, what values absorbed with what concessions, could appear much less important than self-improvement itself. Managed literacy offered a softening of class division without a radical alteration of those divisions [see Miles and Smith]. The topic is touched on by many nineteenth-century novelists, and Emily Brontë's use of it is the less surprising in that while her father was educated at Cambridge, illiteracy lay in the Brontës' recent past and perhaps still in their Irish present. (It was Emily's father who first fixed the family name as 'Brontë', as opposed to the previous variations of Prunty, Brunty and Branty.)

Catherine turns Hareton into a potential husband, sharing with him her culture and then property in the form of the combined estates of Wuthering Heights and Thrushcross Grange. Marriage will now be a healing of Earnshaws and Lintons, and a model of cross-class reconciliation in classic nineteenth-century terms, replacing the conflict of Heathcliff's generation with a new deal. The sensitive negotiation and mutual understanding of Catherine and Hareton overcomes snobbery on the one side, and suspicion on the other. Their marriage is significantly delayed beyond the end of the novel, arranged for the 'New Year', a new era when passion and property will be united in culturally reconciled lovers. Wish-fulfilment is in the air: Wuthering Heights becomes surprisingly akin to a Victorian dolls' house, doors and windows open rather than bolted, vegetable plots replaced by flower gardens, its porridge dotted with primroses – a wendy-house free from oppressive authority (though with Nelly in an acceptable role as the parental servant). Although this ending attempts a social resolution of a social problem, it satisfies formal demands more than it solves the problems of class, gender and property, of human emotion and human aspiration which the novel displays. What Catherine and Hareton's future life at the Grange will be like is invisible to an assessing reader. Hareton, though in a gipsy condition, and in situations often echoing Heathcliff's, *is* still the last of the Earnshaws, the heir whose name is inscribed in stone. *His* is the fairy-tale ending Nelly once promised Heathcliff; but, a mere crypto-gipsy in status and personality, Hareton only has to be *restored* to his estates. To solve Hareton's problems is not to solve Heathcliff's retrospectively.

Wuthering Heights presents property as the condition ensuring that every man's hand is effectively against his neighbour; it extends one of Emily's formulations of the law of nature into an assessment of the hidden violence of property-culture: 'life exists on a principle of destruction; every creature must be the relentless instrument of death to the others, or himself cease to live' [see Gérin, 1971, p. 272]. It is Heathcliff and Cathy who expose that mechanism. And if it is objected that in her essay 'The Butterfly' Emily moved beyond such a view of nature to another, more happy and theologically conformist perspective on natural harmony, one may stress, beyond Heathcliff, the story of Hareton and Catherine.

Brontë is not a schizophrenic novelist torn between romance and social analysis: the social perspective is there in the story of the nameless man and the divided woman – and, if it is anywhere, romance is perhaps best detected in the wishful aspects of the treatment of Hareton and Catherine. Yet Catherine's strategy was a way forward, and one which the nineteenth century strove to take.

References

THE STUDIES listed below are those to which I have referred in the 'Survey' and 'Appraisal' and which I have in practice found helpful in attempting to frame issues in debate about Emily Brontë and *Wuthering Heights*. This listing should be regarded as a set of references and not as a selective bibliography. Details of first publication are normally given. Some entries include details of reprintings in convenient anthologies of criticism to which page references in the present study refer.

Allott, Miriam, 'The Rejection of Heathcliff?', *Essays in Criticism*, VIII (January 1958), 27–47; also in her *'Wuthering Heights': A Casebook*, pp. 183–206 (see below).

Allott, Miriam, 'Introduction', in her *'Wuthering Heights': A Casebook*, pp. 11–36 (see below).

Allott, Miriam (ed.), *'Wuthering Heights': A Casebook* (London, 1970).

Allott, Miriam (ed.), *The Brontës: The Critical Heritage* (London and Boston, 1974).

Anon, 'Patrick Branwell Brontë and *Wuthering Heights*', *Brontë Society Transactions*, VII (1927), 97–102.

Atwood, Margaret, 'Hurricane Hazel', in her *Bluebeard's Egg* (London, 1987), pp. 31–59.

Barclay, Janet, *Emily Brontë Criticism 1900–1968: An Annotated Checklist* (New York, 1974).

Barthes, Roland, *The Pleasure of the Text* (London, 1976).

Bell, Vereen M., '*Wuthering Heights* as *Epos*', *College English*, XXV (December 1963), 199–208.

Blondel, Jacques, *Emily Brontë: expérience spirituelle et création poétique* (Paris, 1955).

Bloomfield, Paul, 'To Breathe Lightning', *Time and Tide*, XXIX (20 March 1948), 304.

Bradner, Leicester, 'The Growth of *Wuthering Heights*', *PMLA*, XLVIII (March 1933), 129–46.

Brick, Allen R., '*Wuthering Heights*: Narrators, Audience, and Message', *College English*, XXI (1959), 80–6.
Brick, Allen R., 'Lewes's Review of *Wuthering Heights*', *Nineteenth-Century Fiction*, XIV (March 1960), 355–9.
Brontë, Charlotte, 'Biographical Notice of Ellis and Acton Bell' (1850), in Emily Brontë, *Wuthering Heights*, edited by Ian Jack (Oxford and New York, 1981), pp. 359–65.
Brontë, Charlotte, 'Editor's Preface to the New Edition of *Wuthering Heights*' (1850), *ibid.*, pp. 365–9.
Buchen, Irving M., 'Metaphysical and Social Evolution in *Wuthering Heights*', *Victorian Newsletter*, XXXI (Spring 1967), 15–20.
Buckler, William E., 'Chapter VII of *Wuthering Heights*: A Key to Interpretation', *Nineteenth-Century Fiction*, VII (June 1952), 51–5.
Buckley, Vincent, 'Passion and Control in *Wuthering Heights*', *Southern Review: An Australian Journal of Literary Studies*, I (1964), 5–23.
Calder, Jenni. *Women and Marriage in the Victorian Novel* (London, 1976).
Cannon, John, *The Road to Haworth: The Story of the Brontës' Irish Ancestry* (London, 1980).
Cecil, David, '*Wuthering Heights*', in his *Early Victorian Novelists: Essays in Revaluation* (London, 1934), pp. 147–93.
Chase, Richard, 'The Brontës: A Centennial Observance', *Kenyon Review*, IX (Autumn 1947), 487–506.
Chitham, Edward, 'Emily Brontë and Shelley', in Chitham and Winnifrith, *Brontë Facts and Brontë Problems*, pp. 58–76 (see below).
Chitham, Edward, *A Life of Emily Brontë* (Oxford and New York, 1987).
Chitham, Edward and Winnifrith, Tom, *Brontë Facts and Brontë Problems* (London, 1983).
Collins, Clifford, 'Theme and Convention in *Wuthering Heights*', *The Critic*, I (Autumn 1947), 43–50.
Cooper, Dorothy J., 'The Romantics and Emily Brontë', *Brontë Society Transactions*, XII (1952), 106–12.
Cott, Jeremy, 'Structures of Sound: The Last Sentence of *Wuthering Heights*', *Texas Studies in Literature and Language*, VI (Summer 1964), 280–9.
Davies, Stevie, *Emily Brontë* (London, 1988).

Dodds, Madeleine Hope, 'Heathcliff's Country', *Modern Language Review*, XXXIX (April 1944), 116–29.
Doheny, John, 'From *PMLA* to *Wuthering Heights*', *Paunch*, XXI (October 1964), 21–34.
Drew, Philip, 'Charlotte Brontë as a Critic of *Wuthering Heights*', *Nineteenth-Century Fiction*, XVIII (March 1964), 365–81.
Dry, Florence, *The Sources of 'Wuthering Heights'* (Cambridge, 1937).
Eagleton, Terry, *Myths of Power: A Marxist Study of the Brontës* (London, 1975).
Eagleton, Terry, *Literary Theory: An Introduction* (Oxford, 1983).
Edgar, Pelham, 'Judgements on Appeal: II. The Brontës', *Queen's Quarterly*, XXXIX (August 1932), 414–22.
Ewbank, Inga-Stina, *Their Proper Sphere: The Brontës as Female Novelists* (London, 1966).
Federico, Annette R., 'The Waif at the Window: Emily Brontë's Feminine *Bildungsroman*', *Victorian Newsletter*, LXVIII (Autumn 1985), 26–8.
Fenton, Edith M., 'The Spirit of Emily Brontë's *Wuthering Heights* as Distinguished from that of Gothic Romance', *Washington University Studies (Humanistic Series)*, VIII (1920), 103–22.
Fine, Ronald, 'Lockwood's Dreams and the Key to *Wuthering Heights*', *Nineteenth-Century Fiction*, XXIV (June 1969), 16–30.
Ford, Boris, '*Wuthering Heights*', *Scrutiny*, VII (March 1939), 375–89.
Foucault, Michel, 'What is an Author?' in Harari, Josué V. (ed.), *Textual Strategies: Perspectives in Post-Structuralist Criticism* (New York, 1979; London, 1980), pp. 141–60.
Gaskell, Elizabeth, *The Life of Charlotte Brontë* (London, 1857).
Gérin, Winifred, 'Byron's Influence on the Brontës', *Keats Shelley Memorial Bulletin*, XVII (1966), 1–19.
Gérin, Winifred, *Emily Brontë: A Biography* (Oxford, 1971).
Gilbert, Sandra M. and Gubar, Susan, *The Madwoman in the Attic: The Woman Writer and the Nineteenth-Century Literary Imagination* (New Haven, 1979).
Girdler, Lew, '*Wuthering Heights* and Shakespeare', *Huntingdon Library Quarterly*, XIX (August 1956), 385–92.
Gleckner, Robert F., 'Time in *Wuthering Heights*', *Criticism*, I (Fall 1959), 328–38.

Goetz, William R., 'Genealogy and Incest in *Wuthering Heights*', *Studies in the Novel*, XIV (Winter 1982), 359–76.

Goodridge, J. F., 'A New Heaven and a New Earth', in A. Smith (ed.), *The Art of Emily Brontë*, pp. 160–81 (see below).

Gose, Elliott B., Jr, '*Wuthering Heights*: The Heath and the Hearth', *Nineteenth-Century Fiction*, XXI (1966), 1–19.

Grove, Robin, '"It Would Not Do": Emily Brontë as Poet', in A. Smith (ed.), *The Art of Emily Brontë*, pp. 33–67 (see below).

Grove, Robin, 'The Brontës: Self-Devouring', *Critical Review*, XXVIII (1986), 70–86.

Hafley, James, 'The Villain in *Wuthering Heights*', *Nineteenth-Century Fiction*, XIII (December 1958), 199–215.

Hatfield, C. W. (ed.), *The Complete Poems of Emily Jane Brontë* (New York, 1941).

Hewish, John, *Emily Brontë* (London, 1969).

Holderness, Graham, '*Wuthering Heights*' (Milton Keynes and Philadelphia, 1985).

Holloway, Owen E., '*Wuthering Heights*: A Matter of Method', *Northern Miscellany of Literary Criticism*, I (Autumn 1953), 65–74.

Irwin, Michael, *Picturing: Description and Illusion in the Nineteenth-Century Novel* (London, 1979).

Jack, Ian (ed.), Emily Brontë, *Wuthering Heights* (Oxford and New York, 1981).

Jacobs, N. M., 'Gender and Layered Narrative in *Wuthering Heights* and *The Tenant of Wildfell Hall*', *Journal of Narrative Technique*, XVI, iii (Autumn 1986), 204–19.

Jordan, John E., 'The Ironic Vision of Emily Brontë', *Nineteenth-Century Fiction*, XX (June 1965), 1–18.

Kavanagh, James H., *Emily Brontë* (Oxford, 1985).

Kenney, Blair G., 'Nelly Dean's Witchcraft', *Literature and Psychology*, XVIII (1968), 255–32.

Kermode, Frank, *The Classic* (London, 1975).

Kettle, Arnold, 'Emily Brontë: *Wuthering Heights* (1847)', in his *An Introduction to the English Novel* (London, 1951), pp. 139–55.

Klingopulos, G. D., 'The Novel as Dramatic Poem (II): *Wuthering Heights*', *Scrutiny*, XIV (September 1947), 269–86.

Kovel, J., 'Heathcliff's Quest: Unconscious Themes in

Wuthering Heights', *Hebrew University Studies in Literature and the Arts*, XIII, i (Spring 1985), 29–42.
Lane, Margaret, 'Emily Brontë in a Cold Climate', *Brontë Society Transactions*, XV (1968), 187–200.
Langman, F. H., *'Wuthering Heights'*, *Essays in Criticism*, XV (July 1965), 294–312.
Leavis, Q. D., 'A Fresh Approach to *Wuthering Heights*', in F. R. and Q. D. Leavis, *Lectures in America* (London, 1969), pp. 83–152.
Livermore, Ann Lapraik, 'Byron and Emily Brontë', *Quarterly Review*, 300 (July 1962), 337–44.
MacKay, Ruth M., 'Irish Heaths and German Cliffs: A Study of the Foreign Sources of *Wuthering Heights*', *Brigham Young University Studies*, VII (Autumn 1965), 28–39.
MacKibben, Robert C., 'The Image of the Book in *Wuthering Heights*', *Nineteenth-Century Fiction*, XV (September 1960), 159–69.
Mathison, John K., 'Nelly Dean and the Power of *Wuthering Heights*', *Nineteenth-Century Fiction*, XI (September 1956), 106–29.
Matthews, John T., 'Framing in *Wuthering Heights*', *Texas Studies in Literature and Language*, XXVII (Spring 1985), 25–61.
Meier, T. K., *'Wuthering Heights* and Violations of Class', *Brontë Society Transactions*, XV (1968), 233–6.
Miles, Peter and Smith, Malcolm, 'Writing, Reading, and Working-Class Culture', in their *Cinema, Literature and Society* (London, 1987), pp. 123–43.
Miller, J. Hillis, 'Emily Brontë', in his *The Disappearance of God* (Cambridge, 1963), pp. 157–211.
Miller, J. Hillis, *'Wuthering Heights*: Repetition and the Uncanny,' in his *Fiction and Repetition* (Cambridge, Mass., 1982), pp. 42–72.
Moody, Philippa, 'The Challenge to Maturity in *Wuthering Heights*', *Melbourne Critical Review*, V (1962), 27–39.
Moser, Thomas, 'What is the Matter with Emily Jane?: Conflicting Impulses in *Wuthering Heights*', *Nineteenth-Century Fiction*, XVII (June 1962), 1–19.
Musselwhite, David, *'Wuthering Heights*: The Unacceptable Text', in Barker, Francis (ed.), *Literature, Society and the Sociology of Literature* (Colchester, 1977), pp. 154–60.

Nelson, Jane Gray, 'First American Reviews of the Works of Charlotte, Emily and Anne Brontë', *Brontë Society Transactions*, XIV (1964), 39–44.
Nixon, Ingeborg, 'A Note on the Pattern of *Wuthering Heights*', *English Studies*, XLV (1964), 235–42.
Ratchford, Fannie E., *The Brontës' Web of Childhood* (New York, 1941).
Reynolds, Thomas, 'Division and Unity in *Wuthering Heights*', *University Review (Kansas City)*, XXXII (Autumn 1965), 31–7.
Sanger, Charles Percy, *The Structure of 'Wuthering Heights'* (London, 1926); also in Gregor, Ian (ed.), *The Brontës: A Collection of Critical Essays* (Englewood Cliffs, 1970), pp. 7–18.
Schorer, Mark, 'Technique as Discovery', *Hudson Review*, I (Spring 1948), 67–87.
Schorer, Mark, 'Fiction and the "Matrix of Analogy"', *Kenyon Review*, XI, iv (Autumn, 1949), 539–60.
Senf, Carol A., 'Emily Brontë's Version of Feminist History: *Wuthering Heights*', *Essays in Literature*, XII, ii (Autumn 1985), 201–14.
Shannon, Edgar F., Jr., 'Lockwood's Dreams and the Exegesis of *Wuthering Heights*', *Nineteenth-Century Fiction*, XIV (September 1959), 95–109.
Showalter, Elaine, *A Literature of Their Own: British Women Novelists from Brontë to Lessing* (London, 1977).
Simpson, Charles, *Emily Brontë* (London, 1929).
Smith, Anne, 'Introduction', in her *The Art of Emily Brontë*, pp. 7–29 (see below).
Smith, Anne (ed.), *The Art of Emily Brontë* (London, 1976).
Smith, David, 'The Panelled Bed and the Unrepressible Wish of *Wuthering Heights*', *Paunch*, XXX (1967), 40–7.
Solomon, Eric, 'The Incest Theme in *Wuthering Heights*', *Nineteenth-Century Fiction*, XIV (June 1959), 80–3.
Sontag, Susan, *Illness as Metaphor* (London, 1979).
Spark, Muriel and Stanford, Derek, *Emily Brontë: Her Life and Work* (London, 1953).
Thompson, Wade, 'Infanticide and Sadism in *Wuthering Heights*', *PMLA*, LXXVIII (March 1963), 69–74.
Traversi, Derek, '*Wuthering Heights* after a Hundred Years', *Dublin Review*, CCII (Spring 1949), 154–68.

Van Ghent, Dorothy, 'On *Wuthering Heights*', in her *The English Novel: Form and Function* (New York, 1953; revised edition, 1967), pp. 187–208.
Visick, Mary, *The Genesis of Wuthering Heights* (Hong Kong, 1958, revised edition 1965).
Ward, Mary, 'Introduction' (Haworth edition, 1900), in Allott (ed.), *'Wuthering Heights': A Casebook*, pp. 103–17 (see above).
Watson, Melvin R., *'Wuthering Heights* and the Critics', *The Trollopian*, III (March 1949a), 243–63.
Watson, Melvin R., 'Tempest in the Soul: The Theme and Structure of *Wuthering Heights*', *Nineteenth-Century Fiction*, IV (September 1949b), 87–100.
Williams, Gordon, 'The Problem of Passion in *Wuthering Heights*', *Trivium*, VII (1972), 41–53.
Willis, Irene Cooper, 'The Authorship of *Wuthering Heights*', *The Trollopian*, II (December 1947), 157–68.
Willson, Jo Anne A., '"The Butterfly" and *Wuthering Heights*: A Mystic's Eschatology', *The Victorian Newsletter*, XXXIII (Spring 1968) 22–5.
Wilson, Romer, *All Alone: The Life and Private History of Emily Jane Brontë* (London, 1928).
Winnifrith, Tom, '*Wuthering Heights*: One Volume or Two?, in Chitham and Winnifrith, *Brontë Facts and Brontë Problems*, pp. 84–90 (see above).
Wion, Philip K., 'The Absent Mother in Emily Brontë's *Wuthering Heights*', *American Imago*, XLII, ii (Summer 1985), 143–64.
Woodring, Carl R., 'The Narrators of *Wuthering Heights*', *Nineteenth-Century Fiction*, XI (March 1957), 298–305.

Index

Allen, Dave, 11
Allott, Miriam, 12, 22, 26, 30, 36–7, 43–4, 94, 100
Amis, Kingsley, 11
Angria, 18
Atwood, Margaret, 14, 94
Auden, W. H., 28
Austen, Jane, 51; *Mansfield Park*, 51–2; *Northanger Abbey*, 51–2

Barclay, Janet, 12, 94
Barker, Francis, 98
Barthes, Roland, 48, 94
Bell, Vereen, 23, 94
Bergman, Ingrid, 11
Bible, 24–5, 30; The Good Samaritan, 70–1
Blackwood's Magazine, 25
Blake, William, 26–7
Blondel, Jacques, 24, 26, 94
Bloomfield, Paul, 31, 94
Bogart, Humphrey, 11
Bradner, Leicester, 25, 28–9, 94
Brick, Allen R., 19, 95
Brief Encounter, 11
Brontë, Anne, 17–19, 28, 95, 99; *The Tenant of Wildfell Hall*, 18, 97
Brontë, Patrick Branwell, 17–18, 22, 28, 94
Brontë, Charlotte, 17–21, 24, 27–9, 32, 35, 44, 70, 95, 96, 99; 'Biographical Notice of Ellis and Acton Bell', 19–21, 95; 'Editor's Preface to *Wuthering Heights*', 20–1, 95; *Jane Eyre*, 18–19; *Shirley*, 70
Brontë, Elizabeth, 17
Brontë, Emily Jane, *passim*; 'The Butterfly', 93, 100; 'Cold in the Earth', 28; 'No Coward Soul is Mine', 28; 'The Two Children', 29
Brontë, Maria, 17
Brontë, Rev. Patrick, 17, 23–4, 69–70, 92
Buchen, Irving H., 90, 95
Buckler, William E., 31, 95
Buckley, Vincent, 26, 37, 40, 44, 95
Bush, Kate, 11
Byron, Lord George Gordon, 26–7, 96, 98; 'The Dream', 27

Calder, Jenni, 87, 95
Cannon, John, 21, 24, 95
Casablanca, 11
Castle of Wolfenbach, The, 52
Cecil, David, 14, 21, 36, 46, 95
Chase, Richard, 42, 95
Chaucer, Geoffrey, 31
Chitham, Edward, 15, 17, 21, 23–4, 27, 95, 100
Chesterton, G. K., 16
Coleridge, Samuel Taylor, 26
Collins, Clifford, 26, 38, 95
Conrad, Joseph, 31
Cooper, Dorothy, 27, 95
Cott, Jeremy, 44, 95

Davies, Stevie, 25, 27, 43, 53, 95
Defoe, Daniel, 31; *Moll Flanders*, 31, 51
Devon Commission, 55
Dickens, Charles, 51; *Bleak House*, 51–2; *David Copperfield*, 51
Dobell, Sydney, 30
Dodds, Madeleine Hope, 29, 96
Doheny, John, 47, 96
Drew, Philip, 18, 96
Dry, Florence, 25, 96

Index

Eagleton, Terry, 13, 15, 21, 49, 96
Edgar, Pelham, 32, 96
Eliot, T. S., 37
Ewbank, Inga-Stina, 21, 96

Federico, Annette R., 37, 96
Fenton, Edith, 26, 96
Fine, Ronald, 40, 96
Ford, Boris, 36, 96
Foucault, Michel, 14, 96
Freud, Sigmund, 40–3

Gaskell, Elizabeth, 21, 96
Genesis, 11
Gérin, Winifred, 16, 25, 27, 54, 69, 93, 96
Gilbert, Sandra M., 13, 27, 35, 39–40, 96
Girdler, Lew, 26, 96
Gleckner, Robert F., 30, 96
Goetz, William R., 37, 97
Gondal, 18, 27–30
Goodridge, J. F., 23, 25, 97
Gose, Elliott B., 23, 46–7, 97
Great Gatsby, The, 31
Gregor, Ian, 99
Grove, Robin, 18–19, 86, 97
Gubar, Susan: *see* Gilbert, Sandra

Hafley, James, 16, 32–4, 97
Harari, Josué V., 96
Hatfield, C. W., 27–9, 97
Haworth, 12, 16, 17–19, 70
Hewish, John, 25, 97
Hoffmann, E. T. A., 25; *Das Majorat*, 25
Hogg, James, 25; *The Private Memoirs and Confessions of a Justified Sinner*, 25
Holderness, Graham, 30, 97
Holloway, Owen E., 25, 97
Horace, 67
Howard, Trevor, 11
Howards End, 52

Ireland, 21, 54–5, 70, 92
Irwin, Michael, 23, 97
Isherwood, Christopher, 28

Jack, Ian, 9, 25, 65, 97
Jacobs, N. M., 31, 80, 97
James, Henry, 52; *The Spoils of Poynton*, 52
Johnson, Celia, 11
Jordan, John E., 44, 97

Kavanagh, James H., 13, 34, 57, 97
Keats, John, 26, 47
Keighley Mechanics' Institute, 24
Kenney, Blair G., 34, 40, 97
Kermode, Frank, 49, 57, 97
Kettle, Arnold, 13, 27, 35, 55, 97
Klingopulos, G. D., 26, 44, 97
Kovel, J., 37, 40, 42, 97–8

Lane, Margaret, 43, 98
Langman, F. H., 31, 37, 44, 98
Leavis, F. R., 49, 98
Leavis, Q. D., 22, 98
Lewes, George Henry, 95
Livermore, Ann Lapraik, 27, 98
Liverpool, 19, 54–5, 70
Luddites, 70

MacKay, Ruth, 25, 98
MacKibben, Robert C., 47, 91, 98
Mathison, John K., 34, 98
Matthews, John T., 47, 49, 98
Meier, T. K., 33, 98
Miles, Peter, 92, 98
Miller, J. Hillis, 25, 29, 49, 98
Moody, Philippa, 37, 89–90, 98
Morgan, Charles, 27
Moser, Thomas, 12, 35–6, 38, 40, 42–3, 98
Mrs Dalloway, 51
Musselwhite, David, 81, 91, 98

Nelson, Jane Grey, 22, 99
Nixon, Ingeborg, 26, 99

Oberon, Merle, 11
Olivier, Laurence, 11

Peacock, Thomas Love, 51; *Crotchet Castle*, 51
Ponden Hall, 24
Pritchett, V. S., 32

INDEX

Prunty, 'Welsh', 24
Python, Monty, 12, 14

Ratchford, Fannie, 28, 99
Reynolds, Thomas, 33, 99
Rossetti, D. G., 37

Sanger, C. P., 21, 99
Schorer, Mark, 44–6, 99
Scott, Walter, 25, 65; *The Black Dwarf*, 25; *The Heart of Midlothian*, 25; *Old Mortality*, 25; *Redgauntlet*, 25; *Waverley*, 25, 65
Senf, Carol A., 12, 28, 99
Shakespeare, William, 26, 41, 96; *Antony and Cleopatra*, 10; *Hamlet*, 26, 37; *King Lear*, 26; *Macbeth*, 26; *Richard III*, 26; *Romeo and Juliet*, 10; *Twelfth Night*, 26; *Venus and Adonis*, 41
Shannon, Edgar F., 24–5, 99
Shelley, Percy Bysshe, 27, 95; 'Epipsychidion', 27
Showalter, Elaine, 21, 99
Simmonds, Bartholomew, 25; 'The Bridegroom of Barna', 25
Simpson, Charles, 24, 99
Skelton, John, 25
Smith, Anne, 35, 97, 99
Smith, David, 43, 99
Smith, Malcolm, 92, 98
Solomon, Eric, 37, 99
Sontag, Susan, 16, 99

Spark, Muriel, 17–18, 99
Spenser, Edmund, 52
Stanford, Derek: *see* Spark, Muriel
Swinburne, Algernon, 30

Thackeray, William Makepeace, 19
Thompson, Wade, 12, 47, 99
Tom Jones, 51
Traversi, Derek, 25, 29, 99
Trollope, Anthony, 51; *Barchester Towers*, 52; *Framley Parsonage*, 51

Van Ghent, Dorothy, 29–30, 32, 36, 41, 46, 100
Visick, Mary, 29, 100
Viviani, Emilia, 27

Walpole, Horace, 51; *The Castle of Otranto*, 51–2
Ward, Mary, 22, 43, 100
Watson, Melvin, 32, 47, 100
Waugh, Evelyn, 51; *Brideshead Revisited*, 51–2
Webster, John, 26
Williams, Gordon, 100
Willis, Irene, 22, 100
Willson, Jo Anne A., 36, 100
Wilson, Romer, 25, 100
Winnifrith, Tom, 12, 21, 95, 100
Wion, Philip K., 37, 40, 42, 100
Woodring, Carl, 34, 100
Wordsworth, William, 26
Wyler, William, 11, 14